Psychic Self Defence
Real Solutions

By Jan Brodie

Psychic Self Defence
Real Solutions

ISBN 1898307 36 9

First published 1995
Reprinted 1996
Reprinted 1997

Cover design by Daryth Bastin
Cover and internal illustrations by Emma McKee

Published by:

Capall Bann Publishing
Freshfields
Chieveley
Berks
RG20 8TF

ACKNOWLEDGEMENTS

Thanks are due to the following people:

To Emma McKee for her generosity in illustrating this book for me at such short notice.

To Julia for proof-reading it.

And to those people who have allowed me to interview them and to publish their personal experiences.

Also by Jan Brodie, published by Capall Bann:

Moon Mysteries
Earth Dance

CONTENTS

INTRODUCTION

The phrase 'Psychic Self-Defence' conjures up images of a battle-scarred hero or heroine fighting to the death against an insurmountable foe of horrific proportions. A thing not of flesh and blood but gestated in another world; an entity of power and threatening reality.

In reality, Psychic Self-Defence is simply having the understanding and confidence to deal sensibly with the entities that dwell on the astral or otherworlds, to protect yourself and your family from what is commonly known as psychic attack and to understand how to deal with people who wish you harm.

Self-confidence and the ability to believe in yourself are the keys to success in all matters of psychic defence.

This book explains how to recognise a psychic attack and how to handle it. How to summon a guardian to protect the home and person. How to cope with psychic attack during magical or circle work. How to banish 'evil' influences. How to hold your own in the Otherworlds or on the Astral levels. How to make protective amulets and talismans. How to strengthen the aura. How to avoid the pitfalls on the occult path. How to increase self-confidence in magical work and visualisation. Meditations and pathworkings designed to increase awareness of the astral levels are also included.

CHAPTER ONE

PSYCHIC ATTACK

A true psychic attack is extremely rare. Firstly, the person initiating the attack would have to be adept in magic or the occult, and secondly would have to despise you enough to warrant the time and effort involved in bringing the attack into being.

We all have runs of bad luck, when everything seems to go wrong. You might wake up one morning and find water pouring through the kitchen ceiling, then three bills arrive in the post. You contact a plumber and when he arrives to survey the damage we experience that heart-sinking feeling of an empty bank account as he mutters, 'tch, tch' and shakes his head theatrically. He has you over a barrel. You have no choice but to allow him to repair the pipe. Ten minutes later you write out a cheque, teeth grinding, and he departs whistling down the path.

You clear up the mess downstairs and eventually set out for the shops. The supermarket is horrendous, there are queues twenty deep at the checkouts, your legs are bruised from an accident with another shopper's trolley and one of your carrier bags breaks as you are loading your things into the car - it is the bag with the eggs in it, of course!

You arrive home and find a message on the answerphone from your son's school. Could you pick him up please, he is covered in spots! Out you go again. Collect the child (who has recovered by the time you get home - it was a heat rash) and try to make a cup of tea. The kettle won't work. You boil the water in a pan on the cooker and then sit down to relax. 'Mum, the cat's been sick on the carpet!' Your blood pressure is now hovering at a dangerous level. Psychic attack? No. Life! We all have runs of bad luck, when nothing seems to go right. Our mistake is not noticing when things are going well. We rather tend to take good luck for granted.

A true psychic attack is so subtle that we may not even notice it happening. At least for quite a while. A strange odour may be noticed that has no obvious cause, but hangs around the home. No amount of air freshener, disinfectant, cleaning and polishing will shift it. It pervades your life with it's presence. The smell is often reminiscent of sewers, corruption or the sweetish odour of rotting meat.

After a while the odour begins to affect daily life, causing upsets, arguments and accusations. You become over-sensitive about it, imagining that other people think you are dirty. Your friends don't visit so often, not because of the smell, but because you are not such nice people any more, you have become touchy and irritable. The add-on effect can be earth-shattering. Psychic attack can wreck marriages, families and lives.

I have been the victim of psychic attack only twice in my life. Once through someone who I believe harboured a grudge against me for some imagined wrong, and once when working with two other people in circle (but that is another story that I will cover later).

The first attack came by way of a thought-form, or created entity. In appearance it resembled an eye, surrounded by waving tentacles. For a week or thereabouts it invaded my dreams, causing poor sleep and restlessness. I became tired and lethargic. It then started to appear when I was awake; if I shut my eyes for a moment, there it was, pulsing and hideous. I would see it out of the corner of my eye when I was reading or watching television.

Things came to a head when I was in the bathroom taking a shower before our weekly circle. The 'thing' was hovering just below the ceiling, watching me and eminating nastiness. This was when I lost my temper. I finished my shower, dressed and went downstairs.

The 'thing' was still close to me, radiating malevolence. I went outside into the garden and it followed, hanging in the air about twenty feet up. Now in the garden I had at that time a rotary clothes line with three arms and a central pole. I clutched two of the arms in my hands and sent pure energy and white light through them into the central pole, down into the ground and then let the energy build before releasing it like a laser back up the pole into the centre of the 'eye'. As I did this I returned it to it's originator. The thought-form shattered, doubled back into itself and then disappeared.

The feeling of peace and relief was tremendous. I never saw or sensed it again. The strange thing was that I never did anything to warrant a psychic attack in the first place. I have never knowingly intended hurt or harm on anyone else in my life.

Psychic attack wraps its tendrils subtly into the very fibre of life itself. It manifests in illness, not always serious, but the victim feels generally unwell, depressed, is quick to anger and tears. The emotions are muddled and stirred up. These effects can continue for long periods of time, or until the victim realises what is happening and rectifies the situation; either by returning the attack to source or by protecting and shielding himself, thereby disempowering the sender.

Of course, there are instances of psychic attack which occur from other spheres, such as vampirism, astral elementals and people who enjoy 'ill-wishing'. These subjects are dealt with in the following chapters.

CHAPTER 2

ELEMENTAL SPIRITS OF NATURE

Not every visualisation of an 'entity' is a bad omen. We often catch glimpses of elemental beings in our homes and whilst outside. They are just there, and going about their own business. They will not and do not generally bother or hinder us in any way. Unfortunately some people are extremely psychic yet untrained and naive. These people will not recognise elementals for what they are and begin to believe their homes are haunted; causing great upset, panic and distress.

Elemental spirits are beings which are composed purely of Air, Fire, Water or Earth. They exist in their own element, being composed purely of it. It is said that elementals have no souls, they breathe, work and sleep just as man does, but when they die that is the end, they are not reborn into a new body. Elementals have no conscience, no instinct of right and wrong. Elemental Spirits do not mix with other spirits of another element or communicate with each other in any way.

Air elementals are called Sylphs and are the rulers of intelligence, communication, inventiveness and quickness. They are the closest to humans in many ways for they breathe air just as we do; they are also the most difficult to work with.

Sylph

In appearance, Air elementals are very similar to humans but lack the weight of a human body. They are slim and ethereal.

Fire elementals are called Salamanders and are the rulers of strength, loyalty, energy and passion. They exist in the element of Fire. In appearance they are long, dry and very clean. Often they appear in the shape of a salamander or may show themselves as a ball or tongue of fire. Fire elementals are often very helpful to humans, but we should remember that fire destroys just as it gives life.

Water elementals are called Undines and are the rulers of the emotions, feelings, compassion, sympathy, receptivity and psychism. Undines are similar to Sylphs in appearance but are more nebulous and fluid; just as water takes on the shape of the vessel that contains it.

Earth elementals are called Gnomes and are the rulers of wealth, stability, practicality, wisdom and preservation. Gnomes are humanoid in shape but are able to alter their size to become giants or to appear small and dwarfish. Gnomes can pass through solid rock with ease. Of all the elemental spirits, Gnomes are the most bad-tempered, this is not to say that they refuse to offer their help and friendship, but they prefer to choose who they will assist or befriend.

Each elemental kingdom is governed by an Elemental King:

Paralda is the ruler of the air elementals
Djinn is the ruler of the fire elementals
Ghob is the ruler of the earth elementals
Niska is the ruler of the water elementals

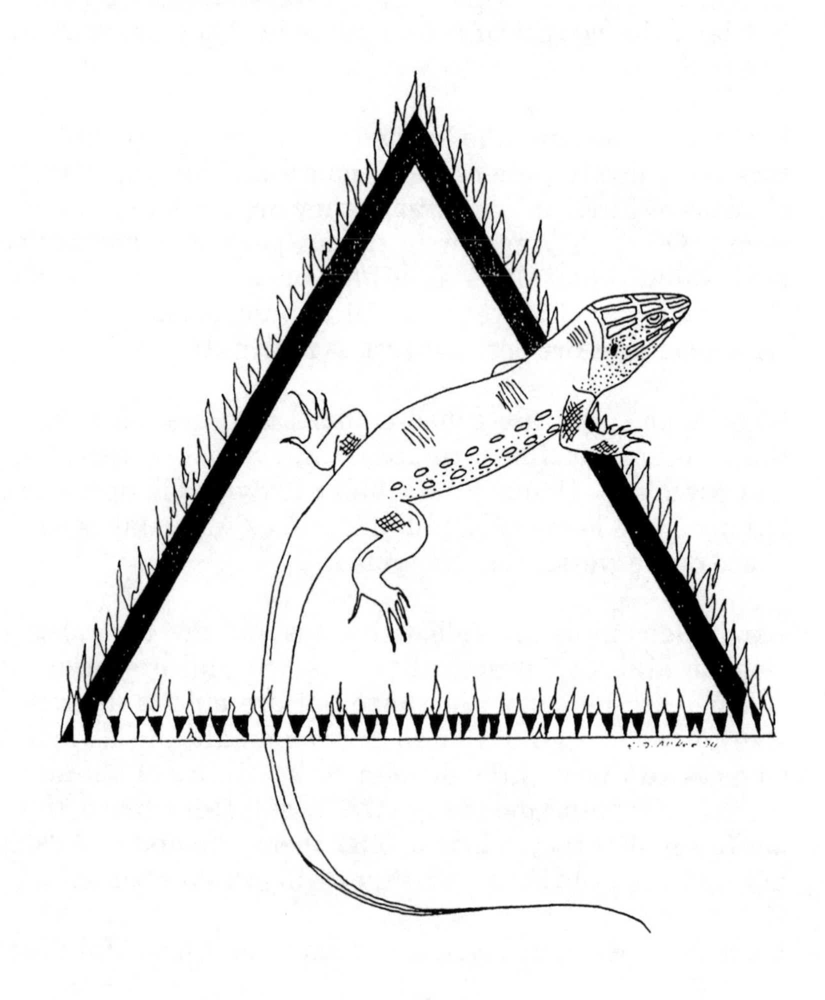

Salamander

The elemental rulers, unlike their subjects, do have conscience. They are intelligent and wise beings and require and even demand the respect due to their station.

Once, several years ago, I was involved in a ritual in which Djinn, the King of Fire, was invoked to assist in a love ritual. This was undertaken with great care and deliberation, one does not call an elemental king unless his presence is absolutely necessary. Djinn appeared and willingly helped us in our work.

However, one of us was rather slow in thanking him for his assistance and the candle used as a focus for the rite began to roar like a bunsen burner with the flame standing four inches high. Djinn was quickly thanked for his time and help with great sincerity and the flame and the roaring died down straight away. Our hands had been well and truly slapped. The kings are proud and arrogant creatures and it doesn't do to ruffle their feathers in any way. If we upset them they will refuse to help us again.

To help with the visualisation of the Elemental Kings, their accepted appearance is as follows:

> Djinn (fire) is composed of living fire, his eyes exude sparks and power.
>
> Paralda (air) appears as a bluish-grey mist. He changes shape like fog.
>
> Ghob (earth) is solid and heavy. He appears Gnomish.
>
> Niksa (water) is mutable and flowing and is the colour of a greenish-blue sea.

Undine

All the Kings pulsate with the energy of their element. On the whole, if elemental spirits trust and like us they are only too happy to assist us in our work. They will lend us their powers and be our friends, but they do like to be asked properly and thanked properly afterwards.

Always treat them with the respect and honour that is their due. Elementals dislike people who are arrogant, greedy, gluttonous and demanding, but they accept people who are generous, kind, giving and thoughtful.

Each elemental type deals with discord in it's own manner. Air works by talking problems over and with persuasion and communication. Fire works by direct confrontation and action. Water wears away problems by erosion or by flowing around and over them. Earth does not give in to a problem, it acts with stubbornness and obstinacy. Earth tends to endure difficulties until they disappear. Earth will also keep chipping away at a problem until it disappears.

We all have an inborn elemental makeup. If you have studied astrology or have had a birthchart erected, you will know that the Sun Sign, Ascendant and Moon Sign are of great importance in the understanding of personality. All the astrological signs are divided up into Earth, Air, Fire and Water. By looking at your own birth details you will easily see which elements are the strongest in your chart; and from that information you will understand the manner in which you will best deal with conflict or psychic attack.

In my own chart I have an Aries Sun, Leo Ascendant and Pisces Moon. My natural reaction is to fight back with anger, (Aries Sun) because my proud and arrogant Leo Ascendant finds it difficult to understand how anyone would dare to attack me (this is not by any means the ideal way, because my Pisces Moon causes me to worry about it later)

Gnomes

The understanding and acceptance of our own elemental strengths and weaknesses is of great importance in any method of psychic self-defence.

The elemental spirits of nature can be called upon to assist and help you in matters of psychic self-defence, but they must not be imprisoned or bound to you in any way. Elementals must be given leave to return to their own realms after each 'working'. If an elemental is trapped in our world, it will react in the only way it understands; by causing chaos involving it's own element. i.e. electrical faults, fires, burns (fire); floods, burst pipes (water); draughts, irritation (air); cracks in walls, things of value disappearing (earth). A few words addressed to the elemental will return it to it's own domain. You could say, for instance:

> SPIRIT OF FIRE, BEING OF STRENGTH. I KNOW OF YOUR PAIN AND IMPRISONMENT HERE. NOW I WOULD RETURN YOU TO YOUR OWN REALM WITH LOVE AND BLESSINGS. ENTER THIS FLAME (light candle) AND DEPART.
>
> (Visualise the spirit returning to it's own world)
>
> IT IS DONE!

Similar words could be used for the other elements, substituting water, earth or incense for the candle.

Bes, the Egyptian Protective God of the Household

CHAPTER THREE

GUARDIAN SPIRITS

A guardian spirit may be invoked to protect the home and its occupants. This spirit is really a visualised and created thought-form that is given life by the constant visualisation of the instigator. A guardian is kept 'alive' for a period of a year and a day (a note must be kept of the date of 'birth' of the guardian as it must be released after that time and another guardian invoked in its place).

The guardian spirit is nearly always an animal or bird of some kind. The animals most often used are tigers, lions, panthers, bears, dogs, dragons and birds such as eagles. I know people who have used a spider successfully and another person who invoked a goose, unusual at first glance - but think about it!

Before performing the ritual to invoke your guardian, allow a couple of days to think about your animal or bird. Often a visualisation will begin to crystallise of its own accord. If you are getting strong images of a bear, for instance, but you quite fancied a dragon (dragons being rather romantic), sorry, but the bear has been chosen for you. You must follow your instincts. If you decided after all, to invoke a dragon instead, that visualisation would rather lack in power and you could not be completely trusting in it.

Now you have chosen your guardian, you must get to know it. See it in all it's varied personalities: friendly, fierce, angry, terratorial, playful and protective. The guardian is your friend not your enemy, it is only the enemy of those who would wish you harm or to rob you of your possessions or damage your home, person or property.

Once your guardian is set (after you work the ritual) speak to it every day and feed it with love and laughter. Like any creature it will thrive on affection and caring. For the year and a day of its existance it is a part of your family. Guardians hate to be ignored.

When your home is to be unoccupied, such as holidays, days or evenings out, call your guardian to defend and guard your property in your absence, and thank it on your return. So not keep your guardian on duty for twenty-four hours a day when you are at home, it needs a little time off too.

About five years ago I went on holiday with my family. The guardian was invoked to watch and protect our home with the proviso that only my mother and a friend (who was to feed our cats) would be able to enter.

On the day before we returned, our friend gave the key to another friend who wanted to retrieve something we had borrowed from him. However much he tried, he could not turn the key in the lock. He brought the first friend with him and she opened the door straight away with no problems.

Guardians do work for you, at least I have found it to be so from my own experience.

HOW TO INVOKE A GUARDIAN SPIRIT

In this rite I have used a dragon as a guardian, but you may substitute your own chosen animal or bird.

Clean the area you have chosen to work in and remove any litter and rubbish. Play some gentle and relaxing music. Light some incense and place this in the East of your room. Place a candle in the South, a small dish of water in the West and a dish of earth in the North.

Turn to face the East and say:

> SPIRITS OF THE EAST, BE WITH ME IN THIS PLACE, LEND ME YOUR POWERS OF THOUGHT, COMMUNICATION AND QUICKNESS. BY THE POWERS OF AIR, LET IT BE!
>
> (Sprinkle some incense on the charcoal)

Turn to face the South, and say:

> SPIRITS OF THE SOUTH, BE WITH ME IN THIS PLACE. LEND ME YOUR POWERS OF STRENGTH, LOYALTY AND ENERGY. BY THE POWERS OF FIRE, LET IT BE!
>
> (Light the candle)

Turn to face the West, and say:

> SPIRITS OF THE WEST, BE WITH ME IN THIS PLACE, LEND ME YOUR POWERS OF EMOTION, SYMPATHY AND RECEPTIVITY. BY THE POWERS OF WATER, LET IT BE!

(Touch your fingers into the water)

Turn to face the North, and say:

> SPIRITS OF THE NORTH, BE WITH ME IN THIS PLACE. LEND ME YOUR POWERS OF STABILITY, PRACTICALITY AND ENDURANCE. BY THE POWERS OF EARTH, LET IT BE!
>
> (Touch your fingers to the bowl of earth).

Sit quietly in the centre of the room and meditate upon your chosen animal. See it as a real, protective force. Smell its odour or scent and allow it to grow in your imagination. When the image is a strong as possible, stand up and say.

> I CALL YOU, GUARDIAN OF PROTECTION. I SUMMON YOU DRAGON OF SAFEGUARD. WATCH THIS HOME AND FAMILY AND DEFEND THEM FROM HARM. LOOK TO ALL QUARTERS WHERE MISCHIEF MAY STRIKE. LOOK ABOVE AND BELOW, INSIDE AND OUTSIDE, WITHOUT AND WITHIN. GUARD THIS PLACE FOR A YEAR AND A DAY, AND FROM THAT TIME HENCE, YOU SHALL BE FREE TO DEPART CARRYING OUR LOVE AND BLESSINGS WITH YOU TO YOUR OWN DOMAIN.
>
> (Visualise the guardian settling in and being at peace with you) LET IT BE!

Thank the Spirits of the Elements, so they may return to their own realms. Turn to the East and say:

SPIRITS OF THE EAST, POWERS OF AIR, I THANK YOU FOR YOUR PRESENCE IN THIS PLACE, DEPART NOW TO YOUR OWN REALM, AND CARRY OUR LOVE AND BLESSINGS WITH YOU. (Thank the spirits of Fire, Water and Earth in the same way, facing the appropriate element.)

After a year and a day has passed, you must release your guardian and then invoke his successor.

TO RELEASE A GUARDIAN

Prepare your working area as previously described and invoke the Powers of the Elements. Visualise your guardian clearly and say:

> I CALL YOU, GUARDIAN OF THE HOME, DRAGON OF PROTECTION. (Sense his presence) I THANK YOU FOR YOUR PRESENCE AND CARE OF THE LAST YEAR AND FOR YOUR WORK WELL DONE. DEPART NOW TO YOUR OWN REALM WITH MY LOVE AND BLESSINGS.
>
> (Feel the presence of your departing guardian leave, and sit quietly for a few moments.)

You may then invoke a new guardian for the coming year.

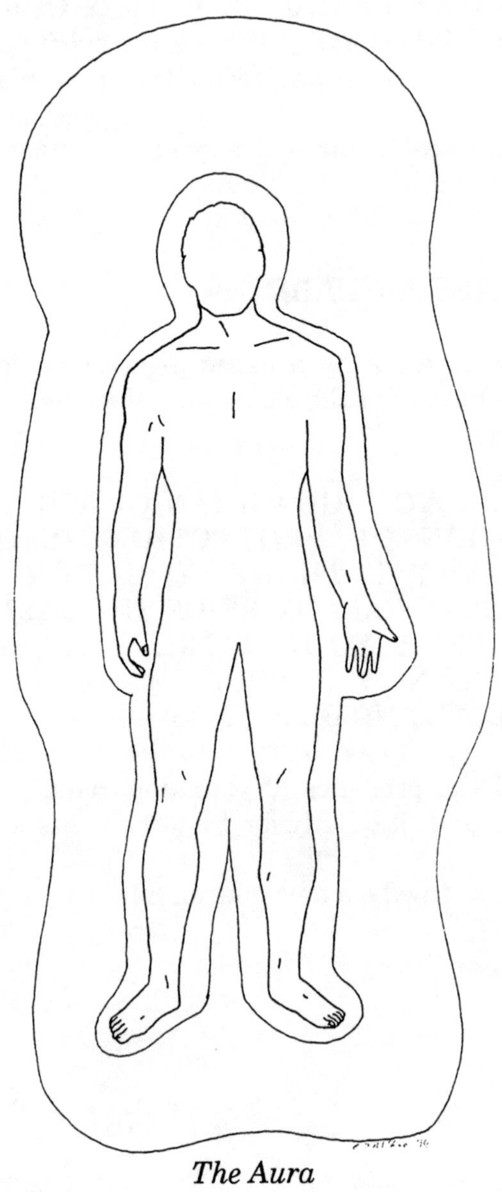

The Aura

CHAPTER FOUR

THE AURA

The Oxford Dictionary describes the Aura as: *A subtle emanation from anything; atmosphere diffused by or attending a person (esp. in mystical use as a definite envelope of body or spirit).*

The aura is an oviform shape that surrounds each and every person. It can be felt by many people and seen by not quite so many. When someone 'invades our space' or stands just that bit too close for comfort, we tend to take a step backwards. We are actually removing that person from the confines of our aura. Our aura is, in a way, an extra sense. It protects our vulnerability, it can warn us of danger, and we are all perfectly capable of strengthening it and utilising it for psychic protection. The aura can act as a force field around the body from which negativity is repelled or bounced off.

Many old religious paintings show the aura as a golden halo around the subject, sometimes surrounding the subject entirely. In fact, the aura is so much a part of spirituality that if you ask a child to draw a picture of an angel, he will draw the aura as well (a halo). The golden aura of the angel is the colour of the higher spiritual and divinity.

The aura has two parts, one lying inside the other, giving the appearance of a double skin. The two parts are known as the Etheric Aura and the Spiritual Aura. The Etheric Aura can extend away from the physical body by some six inches or thereabouts, and appears as a shadowy haze or mist. The Etheric Aura is most easily observed and carries colour. The Spiritual Aura lies outside the Etheric and can extend from a few inches to several feet away from the body. In some cases it may extend for a great distance, especially if the person is highly developed.

Seeing the aura can take practice and time for most people, but we don't have to be able to see it to know it is there. It acts as a barometer to indicate our state of health, whether mental or physical. It shows our degree of spiritual or psychic development and how far our soul has advanced and it forms a protective shield of energy. There is such a thing as a 'false aura' which appears when we stare at a subject for a long time and then move our eyes away. We will then see a colour surrounding the subject. This is not the aura, it is a natural phenomena.

Each colour has it's own complement. If we look at a blue object then at a white piece of paper or wall, we will see orange on the paper. Red is the complementary colour of green and vice versa. Yellow is the complementary colour of violet. Many people, I am afraid, make the mistake of thinking they have seen the aura, but are sadly wrong.

The best situation for glimpsing an aura is when the subject is against a dark background. Dark colours are not reflective so any colours or haze surrounding a person are not going to be tricks of the eye and brain.

The best colours for psychic self-defence are electric blue, clear, pure, white light and violet. The aura can be strengthened by the visualisation of one of these colours surrounding the body. The colour can be controlled through will-power and concentration. The aura can then be drawn in or expanded to your own degree of comfort. If you feel relaxed and comfortable, then your aura will be kept quite close to your physical body. If, on the other hand, you feel uneasy then you can push your aura outwards to give yourself more space. The aura can also be used as a shield or force-field to protect yourself from negative energies.

Imagine that you are going to a busy town centre or supermarket on a Saturday. There will be many people milling about. You set out from home feeling relaxed and happy, looking forward to a pleasant afternoons shopping. After a while you begin to feel edgy and irritated. The feeling of unease and distress grows until you eventually go home in a filthy temper and bite your partner's head off when he asks if you bought anything nice. What has happened is that you have psychically picked up the negative energies flying all around you. All that anger, irritation, bad-temper and general fed-upness emanating from crowds of people has attached itself to you and blossomed.

The aura around the person can be strengthened and protected in several ways. Firstly the aura can be 'polished' until you can visualise it shining like a mirror. Carry that visualisation with you and it will reflect negative energies off its surface.

Secondly, visualise an electric blue or violet cloak and hood, which completely covers the body, preventing it from absorbing negativity, and creating an effective shield.

Thirdly, the body can be enclosed in a bag of protective light, inside which you can move freely and without hindrance.

Fourthly, the aura can be visualised as a pure white light, which slowly crystallizes into a protective shell of protection.

Of these, I prefer to use the 'polishing' method which I have found to be the most suitable and effective for my own purposes, but there are no hard and fast rules about this. Choose the method which you feel offers you the most protection, and with which you feel most comfortable.

The above methods of psychic protection can also be utilised during sessions of clairvoyance when the aura tends to be most vulnerable.

CHAPTER FIVE

THE ASTRAL LEVELS

The Oxford Dictionary defines the Astral as:- *Astral - of stars (astral body - spiritual appearance of the human form).*

Almost everyone has had experience of what is known as the Astral Levels. We dream, and the places we visit and the people and creatures we see during our dreams exist on the Astral Levels. Dreams take many varied forms. Some are the result of worry or tension, some are glimpses of the future or of the past, others are threaded through with strange visions of unknown places.

When we dream we enter a state of astral travel. We leave our bodies and exist for a while in another dimension where anything is possible. We dream about happy and pleasant things, we also dream about terrifying monsters, murder and being chased. Pleasant dreams are relaxing and happy. We awaken contented, rested and peaceful. Often we don't want to wake up but would like to remain in that wonderful place for a while longer.

The Astral Plane exists when we are operating in our Astral Body. This occurs through dreams or through conscious Astral Projection; a state which through practice enables us to leave our physical bodies at will and move upon the Astral Plane quite consciously for a particular purpose. The Astral

Body is the medium in which we travel upon the Astral; just as we use a car to travel on the road, an aeroplane to travel through the sky and a ship or submarine to travel on or under water.

When we sleep, the Astral Body withdraws from the physical body and travels the Astral. The scenery on the astral much resembles that of Earth, but the beings found there are extremely different and often startling and strange.

The occupants of the Astral levels are varied, but in the main consist of 'ghosts' which are simply the astral appearances of people either dead or astral travelling like yourself, human entities, non-human entities, elementals and thought-forms (created images).

The Astral also contains records of everything that has happened in physical life, rather like a video library. These records can be accessed by a person with enough training and understanding to use the key to the library door. Some clairvoyants and mediums are capable of tapping into this library and can achieve stunning 'clairvoyance' through this ability.

The physical human body is three-dimensional, it has length, breadth and depth and can move in three directions: up, sideways left and sideways right. On the Astral the body becomes trans-dimensional and can move freely in any direction including down. It can also change it's shape as circumstances demand.

The astral body is said by many to be attached to the physical body by a silver cord. This is mentioned in the Bible, and it is believed that if the cord is in some way severed the astral body would be unable to return to the physical body. The person would then die, the belief being that one can not exist without the other.

I have found through my own experiences of astral travel, both in dreams and consciousness, that I have had no such cord attached to my body, and I have never experienced difficulty in returning to it. In fact, if I noticed such a cord I would visualise it as being severed, as I can only see it as an encumberance. (This may be partly because I am very ticklish in the area of the navel and would hate to have anything attached to mine!) I have asked many people of my aquaintance if they have a silver cord attached to them when astral travelling and none of them had ever noticed one. Similarily, they have had no difficulty in returning to their physical bodies either.

OCCUPANTS OF THE ASTRAL

GHOSTS

The 'ghosts' that exist on the astral levels are, as I mentioned before, the spirits of dead people or are the projected images of people who are astral travelling like yourself. After physical death the spirit departs to the astral plane. The spirit of an ordinary person will not stay there long, probably only for a few months, until a process of healing and purification is completed.

Good 'souls' are quickly elevated to the higher planes of spirituality. In fact, the decency and goodness of an individuals life and personality on earth is directly reflected in the time he spends on the astral plane after death. The time the spirit spends on the astral is temporary, it just needs to outlast lower and earthly appetites to enable progression to the higher levels. If a person has led a dissolute life, is a liar, a cheat, is violent and brutish and generally evil and unpleasant; his spirit is going to have similar inclinations. He will not suddenly become an angel of mercy after death. That spirit will cheat, lie and enjoy violence and evil after death. The process of cleansing and purification would take many years to accomplish, and a change in his nature much longer. These spirits wander the astral with mischief in mind, they are 'affectionately' known as 'astral headbangers'. (This term intends no disrespect to people who enjoy heavy metal and rock music, of which I have several dear friends.) It is against this type of low spirit that psychic protection is necessary.

Many people have dabbled with ouija boards and have drawn this type of spirit to them, with very unpleasant consequences. It is important to remember that not all spirits tell the truth, they will profess to be whoever you want them to be. It is pointless in saying 'Are you there, Uncle Albert', because 'Uncle Albert' could be someone else entirely and proceed to wreak havoc on your home and family.

The other type of 'ghost' seen on the astral levels are images of other travellers and are just as entitled to be there as you are. Some are people travelling in dream-state and are often unaware of your presence. Others are the images of people who have a very high degree of spiritual development and are adepts of the occult.

If you are challenged by a 'higher soul' be prepared to give way to his or her higher knowledge and understanding. All astral travellers have a certificate of competency which is carried in the aura, a novice might have something like a high street bank cash card; it allows him to access money only. An adept would have the spiritual equivalent of AMEX Gold and unlimited credit.

ELEMENTALS

These non-human entities are cunning, unpleasant, vindictive and dislike humans. They feed on human energies, especially fear and discord. Elementals are not the Elemental Spirits of Nature mentioned in Chapter 2, and they can be drawn into our plane of existence through people who dabble. Elementals can cause dreadful problems through sheer enjoyment of human suffering. Destroy them with a banishing pentacle.

INCUBUS AND SUCCUBUS

The Incubus (male) and Succubus (female) are parasitic elemental spirits which 'glamourise' a human victim. When the human is in their power they will drain him or her of all energy. They appear to be extremely attractive and pleasant, so protection against them is almost non-existent. They appear most often in dreams of an erotic nature. Banish them with a banishing pentacle or refuse to co-operate until they give up.

I have a friend who was kissed by a succubus in a dream. He immediately awoke and could feel the pressure on his lips for an hour afterwards (and this was after he had banished it!)

In medieval times it was believed that Incubi and Succubi were drawn to people who had lewd and immoral thoughts.

THOUGHT-FORMS

A thought-form is a created image which wanders the astral. It can take any shape or size. Thought-forms are sometimes created to attack the astral-bodies of travellers, and can be extremely frightening. Thought-forms are often seen in 'chasing' dreams; when a monster pursues the dreamer, or the dreamer is running away from an axe-wielding madman.

Even when astral-dreaming we have control over events. It is possible to stop a dream and re-play the video, altering the final outcome. A monster can be changed into a harmless, fluffy duckling or other non-threatening creature by the power of your own directed will.

The following exercise is devised to give the astral-traveller arms and armour with which to fight and defend himself upon the astral levels. It effectively shows the strengths and weaknesses of a person and what elemental weapon would be most effective in an attack situation. A crystal may not appear, on first thought, to have the same knock-down power as a machine gun, but on the astral we are dealing with energies and bullets would be useless. That crystal could amplify the power of an earth nature and generate a blast of pure light that would annihilate any adversary.

Things are not always as they first appear. Put your trust and faith into your weapons, they cannot let you down; being created from your own personality.

CREATIVE VISUALISATION TECHNIQUE TO 'ARM' THE ASTRAL TRAVELLER

Ensure that the room which you have chosen for this exercise is warm (but not overheated). Have some peaceful and gentle music playing softly in the background (certain pieces by Delius are extremely atmospheric and conducive to relaxation). Prepare some food and a non-alcoholic drink for 'earthing' yourself with afterwards, a sandwich or biscuit and a glass of water is sufficient. Food and drink bring us back to, and stabilise us on, our own plane very effectively.

You may find it easier to record the visualisation onto tape beforehand and then play it back to yourself during the meditation. It is important, if you choose this method, that you allow adequate time to build up each image before moving on to the next. If you are unable to pre-record the exercise, then read through the passage several times until it is held clearly in your memory.

VISUALISATION EXERCISE

You are walking along a woodland path. The day is warm and a pleasant breeze plays upon your skin as you travel along. The trees and undergrowth are alive with birds and small animals and you hear their voices as you pass by. Brightly coloured butterflies hover and dance in the air. The atmosphere of the wood is calm and peaceful. You are at one with nature. You arrive at a clearing and rest for a while.

At the opposite side of the clearing you see a large rock formation and notice a waterfall which pours into a pool of crystal clarity. The pool is surrounded by rocks and ferns. This a place of idyllic beauty. A cup stands on a ledge of rock and you notice a spring of fresh water nearby. You fill the cup with springwater and drink. The water is cold and sweet upon your tongue, and you are immediately refreshed.

You replace the cup on it's ledge and wander over to inspect the rock formation. You reach out to touch the stone and are surprised to feel a gentle heat issuing from it.

The breeze quickens, but you are not cold. All the elements are here and in harmony. A bush stands isolated in the centre of the rocky outcrop, and you move towards it, curious. You touch the bush and feel the softness of its leaves, and parting its small branches you see an opening in the rock behind it. The opening is just large enough for you to squeeze inside. You manoeuvre your body between the rock face and the bush and enter the opening. It is very dark inside, yet comfortably warm and pleasant.

Although your physical eyes see little, your intuitive eyes are aware of your surroundings. This is a safe darkness, there are no threats, no dangers, no worries. You feel contented and at peace. You begin to move forwards, your feet finding their own path in the enveloping darkness. You become aware that this is a corridor and continue to travel along its length. The corridor ends quite suddenly and you sense that it branches off into two small tunnels, one to the left and one to the right.

You decide to explore the left tunnel first, and begin to make your way along it. The walls are close to your body and feel warm and slightly damp to your touch. The tunnel widens out as you reach the end and you find yourself in an oval chamber. The floor is soft and warm and you sit down quietly. This chamber is the place where you will learn to understand your weaknesses. Here you will admit to the things you fear. Here you will recognise your faults. Nothing can harm you in this place for here are nurtured the seeds of your own personality. Spend some time in the chamber of disempowerment, quietly meditating until to feel you are ready to face the other half of yourself.

You begin the journey away from the oval chamber and return to the tunnel. You feel light and free, as if all the worries and anxieties of your physical person have been lifted from your shoulders. You reach the end of the tunnel and move rapidly towards the opening of the other tunnel, which goes to the right. You enter its confines and once more feel the warm dampness of the walls. You enter the oval chamber and sit upon the welcoming floor. In this chamber you recognise the good and positive things about yourself. Here you see your attributes, your gifts and your empowerment. Here are your strengths and abilities. Rejoice in them, they are your confidence and your armour. Sit for a while in the chamber of empowerment and let its energies build within you.

When you are ready you stand and leave the chamber, feeling positive and uplifted. You re-enter the tunnel and travel down it until you find yourself once more at the entrance to the corridor. The corridor is no more, and a large pear-shaped room lies in its place. You are standing at the widest part. You move forwards until you are in the centre of the room and then pause. You notice a reddish light permeating the walls, filtering through. Once more you sit down on the welcoming floor. This is the hall of arming, and it is here your astral weapon will be bestowed upon you. Think carefully and quietly about your own elemental makeup and of your powers and weaknesses. Open your eyes and you will see before your weapon. Reach out and take it. Your weapon may be a crystal of earth or a sword of light. It may be a cup of water or a vessel of curling mist. It may be anything. Whatever it is, it holds power and can be used in your defence. Believe in it.

You stand up and move towards the narrower part of the room, which once more becomes a corridor. Now you must empower your symbol of divinity. Visualise your symbol, be it a pentacle, a cross, a Star of David, a tree branch, a bird or whatever. See it shining and pulsing with pure white light. It stands at the entrance to the outside world. You walk towards it and then pass through it, absorbing it into your body. You feel its protective aura knit with your own.

You squeeze through the bush and are once more in the clearing. The sun warms your face and the breeze plays gently on your skin. You return to the spring and once more take the cup and drink. Before you stands a door. You open it and see your own room and yourself on the other side. You enter the room and are home. Allow yourself time to become aware of your surroundings, and when you are ready open your eyes.

If you experience difficulty in 'earthing' yourself properly afterwards; stamp your feet on the floor a few times before taking a drink and eating your prepared food.

CHAPTER SIX

THE PSYCHIC VAMPIRE

Psychic Vampires tend to fall into two main categories; the innocent and the amoral.

The innocent or unwitting psychic vampire is unaware of his or her vampiristic tendancies. These people are extremely draining and we become wearied after spending time in their company. They drain the energies of the people they come into contact with. Unfortunately, these types will be drawn towards those who can give them the boosts of energy they need. 'I love to visit you', they say 'your house is always so peaceful, and I always feel better when I have been talking to you. I don't know why, but I seem to be drawn here when I am feeling down.' He or she is telling the truth, you do make them feel brighter and more confident; you are feeding their failing vitality with yours!

Old people benefit from being in the company of energetic children and teenagers. I have seen a person in his eighties visibly shed ten years after spending an hour with youngsters. He became more alert, regained his sense of humour and was much more agile; whereas previously he had been sitting in his chair, miserable and dozing.

This is not necessarily a situation to be avoided; we give our energies freely to those people we love and care for, and this is how it should be. When you are placed in either of the above-mentioned situations, a few moments spent in strengthening your aura is always beneficial.

It has always been said that children and old people should not sleep together in the same room. The old person will steal vitality from the young while asleep. This is nearly always unintentional, but nevertheless very real. If such a situation is unavoidable, then an envelope of light should be placed around the child for protection. I place such a protection over my children every night as a matter of course, and they have very rarely suffered from 'bad dreams'.

One of the most dangerous types of psychic vampire is the so-called 'best friend'. Most often this person is female, and a very feminine type of female. She appears to be pleasant, friendly, sweet, calm and innocent. She shows herself as being concerned for your welfare and as being completely incapable of inflicting hurt on anyone. She is amoral and evil and inside her gentle exterior writhes a demon of anger, jealousy and malice.

She quietly destroys your faith in other people with a careful word placed here and there to create doubts in your mind about their integrity and affection for you. She speaks to them too, on the pretext of friendship, and fires her arrows of suspicion into their subconscious. She is very plausible and people believe her tales.

When you wake up to the situation and confront her, she denies everything with tears in her eyes. You almost feel sorry for her. Your friends (not so friendly now) think you have turned against them and start to protect themselves, or possibly attack you psychically. You begin to feel the effects and return the negativity to the sender. They retaliate and very soon a vicious circle has been created, which can continue endlessly, until the truth comes to light. By that time you feel so hurt that your one time friends could turn against you that the good relationship you once had is truly dead and buried.

She telephones to enquire about your health. 'I couldn't get you out of my mind', she says 'Have you been ill? I lit a candle for you.' She is really asking you if her ill-wishing has worked!

Worry will only increase the problem. She feeds on negative energies. Try to cultivate an atmosphere of lightness and laughter. When she phones, say that everything is fine and you have never felt better. Lie through your teeth if you can. Never let her see she is winning.

This type of vampire is often in poor health, or has a psychological condition. She may be jealous of your abilities, your friendships, your work or business, or your superior understanding of spiritual or magical matters. What is so sad is that you may have welcomed her as a friend, held her hand along her chosen path and supported her through her troubles and anxieties. You may even have taught her how to use the magical weapons she attacks you with!

Cut her out of your life completely and then forget about her. She is not worth anything, certainly not your sympathy and regret. If she continues to attack, reflect everything back to her without compunction. You are the one who has been wronged.

THE SICK ROSE

O rose, thou art sick!
The invisible worm
  That flies in the night
In the howling storm,
Has found out thy bed
Of crimson joy,
And his dark secret love,
Does your life destroy.

(William Blake 1757-1827)

There is another type of psychic vampire who sucks energy and vitality from other people. This sort of person attaches herself most often to spiritual or psychic groups. She shows herself as being charming and pleasant to everyone, but weaves a spell over members of the opposite sex, who are her victims.

She is like a human succubus and glamourises men into enthrallment. They can see no harm in the person and are flattered by her devotion, and the way she hangs onto their every word. She touches her victim often and he is left feeling drained and empty. Her aura is muddy and flashes with spurts of fire. Other women feel uncomfortable in her presence and do not like her close to them. There are men in this category also who can glamourise women in the same way. Always, their own sex dislikes them.

These people should be expelled and forgotten for they bring nothing but disruption, trouble and ill-will. They can not cause harm unless they are close to their victim, but can feed on negative energies generated by others which increase their power, as well as on the vitality of their prey.

Psychic vampires are drawn to healers. What better person could there be than a healer who is offering vitality and energy with no conditions attached. During a healing session the healer allows his feelings of love and restoration to flow freely into his 'patient'. A problem can arise when the 'patient' sucks out more energy than is necessary and attaches himself to the healer like a leech, only falling off when he is satiated. The healer will then become drained, tired and possibly disorientated.

A trained healer will know and understand how to protect himself and his aura during sessions of healing. He will not allow himself to become drained. A trained healer is very much aware of this occurrence and its dangers. Many people are gifted, natural healers but should also be aware of the fact that not all 'patients' are honest or nice people. Healing energy should be tempered with a psychic shut-off valve which prevents too much energy being drawn from source.

Not all 'healing vampires' are aware of their condition, they just enjoy the high that healing gives them and so keep on returning for their 'fix'.

I once knew a person who would visit a busy town centre regularly, so she could sit down on a bench and suck energy from passers by or from people who were unfortunate enough to sit down beside her. She did this because she could. Not a nice thing to do, and not a nice person either!

CHAPTER SEVEN

THE REALM OF FAERIE

A HOUSE BLESSING

St. Francis and St. Benedight,
Bless this house from wicked wight,
From the nightmare and the goblin,
That is hight Good-Fellow Robin,
Keep it from all evil spirits,
Fairies, weasels, rats and ferrets,
  From curfew time
To the next prime.

(William Cartwright, 1611-1643)

On the whole, psychic attack from the Realm of Faerie is rare, yet it does exist. I have been asked for advice in ridding people of an 'infestation' only twice in a great many years. Yet when an attack happens it is extremely unpleasant for the people involved.

Ancient manuscripts from the Middle Ages tell of attacks on humans by goblins. The recommended 'cure' in those days was to pray to as many saints as possible and call on the Trinity for help. Names of Divinity carried great weight in those days, and can do so today; if your belief and faith in them is truly strong.

The type of manifestation which is most troublesome is the Imp, Bogle, Wight or Dark Elf. They are classed on the whole as evil goblins, as distinction between them is difficult to make. The dictionary definition of 'Imp' is small devil, spawn of satan.

When Imps appear to humans they can be alarming to see. They have long, thin limbs, are pot-bellied and most often brown or black in colour. They delight in mischief and in frightening and tormenting humans. Imps are prone to swarming, that is they tend to appear in groups and packs, and then cause havoc.

In many cases they will steal or move property and frighten pets. They sometimes break crockery and ornaments. I heard of one attack when Imps crawled over a person's face and scratched and pinched the flesh, causing much distress.

Imps can sometimes be placated by the offering of gifts and a polite request for them to depart. Gifts of food (sweet and sugary) alcohol and silver coins have been known to work in ridding a home of them.

Tonal vibration will drive Imps away, especially high-pitched sounds such as the sound effected when a wet finger is run around the rim of a wineglass.

I was contacted by someone once who had resorted to running a hairdryer inside a metal biscuit tin in an attempt to drive out an infestation of Imps. This method of defence did work in that case. The person involved then fumigated the house with an incense specially formulated to repel them and to prevent their return. Imps dislike certain perfumes and these will effectively keep them away. Formulas for incenses can be found in Chapter 12.

CHAPTER EIGHT

PSYCHIC ATTACK THROUGH WILL POWER AND THE 'EVIL EYE'

This type of attack tends to happen to people who lack in self-confidence and are easily frightened. In a way they bring it upon themselves because of their own fear and doubt. Attack through will-power is effective because the person 'under attack' believes that the attack is real, and because of that belief things will begin to happen or go wrong.

Certain people who work in occult or magical fields have an undeniable charisma about them. They exude power, confidence and an air of 'I know what it's all about and exactly where I'm going.' This type of strong personality can, in effect, scare lesser mortals half to death. They almost want to be under the influence of this person and feel they could have no possible defence against him.

The truth is, that the 'all powerful one' probably has no interest at all in the person 'under attack,' and the things that are going wrong are the result of created thought forms from the victim's own imagination.

I have been accused of 'looking at people' in the past and on my part it has been totally innocent. I was told once 'that the eyes of a Priestess in repose can be truly terrifying' and

I believe this to be true. We learn to shield our eyes because people are afraid of what we may see in theirs.

There are people who enjoy frightening others and there are those who through the power of their will are able to convince others that they wish them harm.

Some even threaten to bring harm on a person and his family if you cross them. This type will make sure you understand that they are attacking you. They will tell you so, write letters and behave in a threatening manner. This is their weakness for their power lies in your belief in their ability. A person with real occult power would not have to tell you anything - he would just destroy your life completely and you wouldn't know it was happening until it was too late.

Deal with psychic bullies by ignoring their threats. Refuse to be undermined. Look them straight in the eye and stare them out. Force yourself to be unafraid and treat them with the contempt they deserve. Think of them in the same vein as you would a chain letter, the type that tells you to send £1 to ten different people or you will die, tear them up and throw them in the dustbin. Then get on with your life!

CHAPTER NINE

GHOSTS

'Ghosts' or apparitions fall into several different categories. The first classification is the type of ghost which haunts a particular place or area, such as the apparition of Anne Boleyn which is believed to haunt the Tower of London. In general a ghost of this nature is an earthbound spirit which is trapped on earth after death. Death has often been of a violent nature, either through murder or accident or the spirit is not aware that it's physical body is actually dead.

People who have been very materialistic during life sometimes have difficulty in letting go of property after death. They do not realise that they are dead, becoming very confused and upset when they see a stranger in their home, changing things. The spirit may then create havoc in the only way it can; by moving or breaking things or appearing as an apparition to those who are sensitive enough to see it. The ghost is bewildered, the people panic and a vicious circle is created.

I would not advise any untrained person to attempt to exorcise a trapped spirit; the process requires the gentle understanding of a medium, who has the ability to send the spirit into the astral light with love and protection. Communication is of the utmost importance.

I am not a Spiritualist, but I have witnessed an exorcism (which the Spiritualists refer to as Rescue Work) in the company of two gifted Spiritualist mediums, and the whole process was effected with love, understanding and consideration to both the trapped spirit and the person whose home was affected. There was no 'casting out' of the spirit, but he was gently told that he was dead and made to understand that he must move on into the light, where he would be met by a loved one. The whole thing was extremely moving and I have nothing but praise for the two mediums involved. The process took about an hour and a half, and the family have not been troubled since.

Spiritualist mediums and healers, I understand, undergo a period of two years training in this kind of work and are, therefore, extremely well qualified to deal with the problems of a 'haunting.' If you need help, contact your local Spiritualist Church and ask for advice; no-one will laugh at you or disregard your story in any way. I have always found them to be both efficient and helpful.

There have been many incidents reported of people either seeing the apparition of, or dreaming about, a person close to them, and then hearing that the person had actually died at the time their image was seen. These are known as Moment-of-Death Apparitions, and this type of manifestation is very difficult for a sceptic to disregard.

When people care about each other, a psychic link is often forged which can span many miles (sometimes many hundreds of miles). I do not pretend to understand why this can happen; whether the dead person visits the loved one, or whether the loved one suddenly feels a strong sensation of the person far away. Whatever it is that causes this phenomena to manifest, it is nevertheless very real. Of course, not every feeling we have about a person means they have died, but there is usually something, which may be as small as a cut finger which forges that psychic link.

When I was fifteen, I went on holiday with a friend and her parents. During my stay I dreamed that my Grandfather was floating on a sea which was covered in flowers of every colour. I found on my return home that he had died that night. The dream, in a way, took away the shock and eased much of my grief.

There is another manner of 'haunting' which is triggered by what I can only describe as a video replay of an event which has occurred in the past. Some people can, through their own psychic vibrational energies, press the replay button and watch the film. When this effect occurs unintentionally, it can cause a person to believe that there is either a ghost or that they are being attacked, when in fact they are standing in the right place at the right time, with the right atmospheric conditions for this phenomena to manifest.

There is a place on Anglesey called Bryn Cellhi Dhu; the ruins of an Iron Age village. I have sat quietly there, amongst the stones and seen visions of the ancient Celts, going about their daily business and I have heard both their voices and their singing. This has happened only twice, when atmospheric conditions have allowed it. At other times I have neither seen nor heard anything.

CHAPTER TEN

PSYCHIC ATTACK DURING CIRCLE WORK

The magical circle, such as is drawn in any Wiccan or Pagan rite, is an actual barrier which protects against evil influences, bad spirits and anything malignant which may try to infiltrate circle work. It is a defence and protection for those who are within its boundary and is composed of the energies of light and love. Psychic attack in these circumstances should not happen. Unfortunately it can and occasionally does.

I was once working with two other people within a properly drawn circle. The working was particularly to help a woman who had asked us to remove a psychic attack which was troubling her a great deal. She was experiencing nasty smells and the manifestation of an unpleasant thought-form. We decided to do what we could to relieve her suffering. The work of the evening began and all progressed smoothly. We attuned to her situation and visualised her without much difficulty. Then we proceeded to try to remove the problem for her.

From upstairs we heard the terrified scream of a child. One of us immediately broke the circle and galloped upstairs to find all the children soundly asleep and peaceful. Back downstairs, he opened the circle, re-entered and closed the circle behind him immediately. It was too late, something was in there with us. (Shades of Dennis Wheatley, you might say, but this is true!) It had entered the circle the moment it had first been broken and waited until we were all together. Then it attacked. One of us was 'stabbed' between the shoulder blades, one in the calf and the other was 'garotted'. We joined hands and stood in a triangle, facing outwards and combining our wills managed to force the entity away. It went eventually, but the experience was most unnerving. We banished the circle immediately.

On the telephone later we demanded to know exactly what had happened to bring the attack on the person who had asked for help in the first place. We found out too late that this attack was in retaliation for a great wrong that she had done to someone else. This someone else was skilled 'in the art of magick'. Our interference had almost cost us dearly. From that experience we learnt a valuable lesson; not to believe everything we are told. There are two sides to every story.

Many people on hearing that you work magic, for instance, will say anything to get you to help them. They will lie or fabricate things, they will give you a misguided impression of their circumstances, they will be completely dishonest in order to try to involve you in their personal wrangles. Never do anything without careful thought and great and serious consideration. It may rebound on you.

Someone once asked us if we could arrange for her husband to have an accident, preferably fatal. We told her that we were not in that line of business, but she could always hire a hitman if she was that desperate. Some people are unbelievable!

Before anyone works in a magical circle for the first time, they should know and understand how to protect themselves. Psychic self-defence should be the first lesson of any novice and it should be learned well. If a person goes into circle feeling in control and confident, then they will at least be capable of avoiding a difficult or possibly nasty situation; or if a difficult situation does come about they would be able to deal with it.

I have sometimes noticed 'watchers' standing on the outside of the circle during a working. They have not interfered in any way, but I prefer not to be watched as any magical working should be private to those who are involved. A banishing pentacle will send them away. These days, I generally draw the circle right up to the walls so they cannot enter the room at all. I have been a 'watcher' myself, purely by accident.

On one occasion I was using a candle for scrying and I found myself watching events in someone else's temple. I saw a door with two snakes on it. The door opened and I saw three figures (complete strangers) inside the room; two women and a man. They were wearing natural coloured woollen robes and were involved in a dance or ritual. Their guardian appeared in the doorway and he looked very much like E.T. with long, gangly arms and a large head. He looked at me and then trotted off. No-one seemed to be aware of my presence and after a while I left.

I thought nothing more about until I had a phone call from someone in the North of England. He had got our number from a mutual friend. We were talking and during the conversation he mentioned that his coven wore robes of damascus wool. The bells began to ring in my head and I asked a few questions about the door, the guardian and the dancers. 'Oh, s***', he said, put the phone down and never rang again. The whole episode should not really have happened and was completely unintentional. I expect he strengthened his seals afterwards, because I have not been back since.

During circle work, there are often strange manifestations, odours, shadows and reflections which are created purely through the power of the ritual. These are not threatening or dangerous in any way, but part of the tapestry of magic. Anything evil, if it got through, would be accompanied by a strong sense of foreboding and disquiet. You would know it was there. Automatic protections would go up and the group would immediately act as one person, linking hands and building protective power to repel and destroy the potency of the invader.

Evil attacks through the weakest link and this is why a thorough knowledge of self defence is so important. Understanding bestows confidence, and confidence properly directed can and will move mountains.

CHAPTER 11

TALISMANS, AMULETS AND CHARMS

The Oxford Dictionary definition of Charm is; *Words or acts or objects having occult power. Trinket resembling amulet. Subject to a spell; bewitch; protect by magic.*

There are many methods of protecting the home, self and family from psychic attack and the use of psychic self-defence in protecting the same from physical attack, such as burglary, criminal damage or assault. Charms, Amulets and Talismans fall into this category. A charm is an object which is made, written or created to bring about or prevent a particular phenomenon or event. Charms can be extremely simple or very elaborate but they are always charged with intent for the particular use they are composed for.

A charm may be as simple as a lucky stone or it may be as complex as a waxen image used in healing. A charm may be in the form of a cloth bag stuffed with specific herbs that influence and encourage the powers of protection. How many of us wear jewellery which incorporates a lucky birthstone or a stone of protection? Quite a few, I would imagine. We also wear the symbols of our spiritual belief; pentacles, crucifixes, six-pointed stars to name but a few. Without our protective spiritual symbol we feel naked and vulnerable.

Stones, whether they be precious or semi-precious have been long-believed to hold particular and protective properties. The following selection of stones can all be utilised in psychic protection.

Agate	Protects against ill-wishing and danger.
Amethyst	Guards against danger. Protects during dreaming.
Amber	Strengthening.
Apache Tear	Protects from danger and harm.
Blue Agate	Calms disturbances.
Carnelian	Stops ill-wishing and negativity.
Chalcedony (Black)	Wards off psychic attack.
Chrysoprase	Shields wearer from negativity.
Crystal Quartz	Can be charged as a psychic weapon.
Flint	Very protective (see hag stones)
Jade	Protects wearer from enemies.
Jasper (Red)	Strengthens defences, sends negativity back to source.
Lapis Lazuli	Spiritual. Wards off attack.
Obsidian	Reflects attack back to source.
Peridot	Darkens when there is danger.
Smokey Quartz	Absorbs evil and negativity into itself. Cleanse very often.

Wear the stone of your choice or carry in a pocket so its protective energies are close to you. Keep larger pieces in your home so they can radiate their vibrational forces freely.

Stones and crystals need to be kept clean so they may be most efficient. People feel brighter and more energetic when they have taken a shower or washed. Crystals feel the same.

It is doubly important that Smokey Quartz is cleaned daily. It attracts negativity and dross like a crystal garbage disposal unit. Very useful, but can get psychically 'whiffy' if neglected.

Crystals can be cleansed by:

a) Burying them in a bowl of rock salt and leaving them there for a couple of hours.

b) Immersing them in a bowl of spring water with a tablespoonful of rock salt dissolved in it; again leave the crystal immersed for a couple of hours or overnight.

c) Holding the crystal in or under running water for a few minutes. Crystals appreciate a gentle scrub with a soft brush and a mild detergent every couple of days. This keeps them fresh and removes the accumulations of dust that gather very quickly.

d) Fume the crystal in the smoke of smouldering sage leaves.

Obsidian and Flint are very effective in psychic self-defence. Obsidian is a naturally occurring volcanic glass and has a highly reflective surface. It has long been used in magic, often as a scrying mirror. It can reflect negative energies and ill-wishing back to source.

I have an obsidian spear head which is used as a protection in my home. If I feel the presence of an attack I point the spear head in the direction I sense the attack comes from and allow it to work for me. It can also be spun to protect our home from all directions.

Hag Stones are equally useful. A hag stone is a pebble with a naturally occurring hole in it. Hag stones are often of flint, which gives double protection. These stones have always been considered lucky as well as protective. They can be found on many beaches throughout the British Isles. Small ones can be worn on a cord around the neck. Many people attach one to their key rings. Larger stones can be nailed to the boundary fences of your property as an added safeguard.

SIX STONES CHARM

Take a pebble from each of the farthest corners of your garden (two from the front and two from the back) and one from outside the front door and one from outside the back door. Do not wash them. Hold them in your hands and will protective energy into them.

Place the stones in the centre of a circle of red cloth and then gather the cloth up to make a bag. Tie the neck with cord and then hang up or place at the point nearest the centre of your property.

To protect the thresholds of property, such as doors and windows; take two pins and cross them in an X shape and place under the carpets and on the window sills, charging them with protective energy as you proceed.

AMULETS

An amulet is a thing that is worn as a charm against evil. Spiritually symbolic jewellery, hag stones and crystals fall into this category, as do mystical symbols or runes carved or etched onto wood or metal. I know people who carry little bags of lucky and protective items with them at all times to ensure protection.

TALISMANS

A talisman is an object endowed with magic powers, especially of averting evil or bringing good luck to its holder. Talismans are often inscribed on paper or parchment and kept in a secure place or kept on an altar. Talismans are made to influence a particular desire or purpose; such as to protect a car or a person from physical or psychic attack. They are very personal and are usually inscribed with the name of the originator together with signs and symbols pertaining to the desired effect required.

Runic talismans are often made from green wood because in the act of cutting the wood from the living tree, the runemaster could ask the tree spirit to lend its power to the talisman, thus increasing its potency.

It is believed that a carefully constructed talisman contains a spirit or spirit force or is in contact with powerful forces which will help the maker to achieve his desire. In this book we are dealing with talismans which will give us protection from negativity and psychic attack.

When you create your talisman, by either cutting, etching or drawing it on parchment or paper, you must be aware that you are imbuing it with power for a particular purpose.

Talismans should not be made for something to do or for a laugh. Utter concentration is of supreme importance as is the strength of will needed to make the talisman fully effective.

When your talisman is completed and blessed you can carry it with you in a wallet to keep it safe and clean. Alternatively you may wear it attached to a cord if it is constructed of a suitable material, such as wood or metal. When the talisman has 'done its work', such as protecting you from an attack by a particular person, it must be either buried in the ground or burnt to ritually set free the spirit within it.

HOW TO MAKE A SIMPLE TALISMAN

Take a piece of 'virgin' parchment or thick paper (I have a large sheet of cotton 'paper' which I keep for talisman making) and cut out a two inch square. This square will become your talisman.

If, for instance, you feel psychically threatened by, say, Peter Jones, and you feel he has been sending ill-will towards you. Then write upon one side of the paper, something like "PETER JONES. YOU CAN NOT HARM ME. YOUR POWER IS NOTHING. I AM SAFE AND STRONG."

As you write visualise Peter Jones failing to affect you, weak and helpless. Turn the paper over and draw on the other side a picture or symbol which you feel gives you strength and protection from his influence. This may be a simple drawing of a sword, held upright, or two fingers making the 'victory' sign; or you may choose something rather more elaborate.

When you have made your talisman, bless it with water, salt, incense smoke and then pass it quickly through a candle flame (you don't want to set it on fire). Talismans should be created within the confines of a protective circle. You could use the elemental protection circle described in Chapter 3 if you are not conversant with Wicca or another magical or spiritual tradition.

Your talisman could also be burnt or carved into wood, or etched or inscribed onto metal, such as copper, silver or pewter and then worn attached to a cord around the neck.

RUNIC TALISMANS

These are usually carved or burnt into wood or etched into metal and then worn around the neck on a cord.

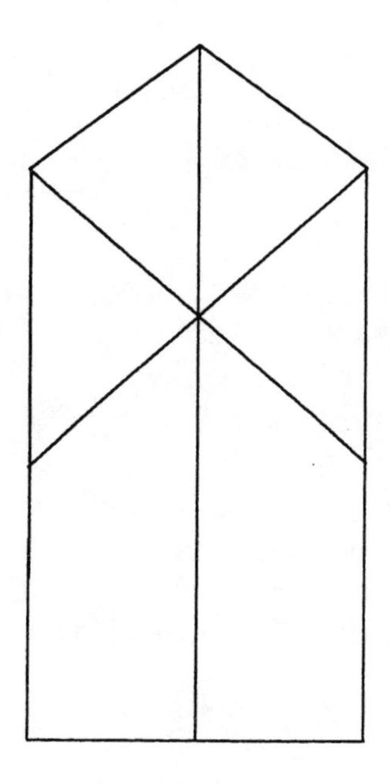

CHAPTER 12

INCENSES, HERBS AND PLANTS

The following herbs and plants can be utilised in the preparation of incenses and charms which will protect against psychic attack. The greater part of these herbs are easily available either from supermarkets, health food shops or from your own garden. Gums and resins may be purchased at a reasonable price from New Age suppliers, herbalists or by mail order (addresses listed at the end of the book).

AGRIMONY

(Agrimonia Eupatoria) The magic and protective power of Agrimony is mentioned in an ancient British manuscript:

> "If it be leyd under mann's heed
> He shal sleepyn as he were deed;
> He shal never drede ne wakyn,
> Till fro under his heed it be takyn."

ANGELICA

(Angelica Archangelica) Angelica is linked to the aegis of Archangels, particularly Michael. It is effective against enchantment, spells, and evil spirits. Use the stems and leaves.

ANISE
(Pimpinella anisum) Anise is a herb that protects against the 'evil eye'. Use the seeds in incenses or sachets.

ASAFOETIDA
(Ferula foetida) also known as Food of the Gods or Devil's Dung. Asafoetida has an extremely offensive smell when burnt. Use in eradication or extermination incense, and never in an enclosed space. Part used is the gum resin obtained from the roots.

BASIL
(Ocymum basilium) Purifying and cleansing. The name is said to be derived from 'basilisk', a mythical creature that could kill with a glance. In ancient times the plant was linked with scorpions; a sprig left in a pot was said to eventually turn into a scorpion. In fact it was believed that just sniffing the plant was enough to cause a scorpion to grow in the brain. Basil has a disinfectant quality, it purifies an impure atmosphere. Use the leaves and stems.

BAY
(Laurus nobilis) Bay is used for exorcism, cleansing, to fight psychic attack, for protection and for curse-breaking.

BENZOIN
(Styrax benzoin) Antiseptic and purifying. Use in cleansing and protection incenses. Part used is the gum resin.

BETONY
(Stachys Betonica) Betony is powerful against evil spirits, it was once planted in churchyards or hung around the neck as a charm to protect against 'fearful visions'. Betony was employed to drive away devils and nightmares. It is protective against psychic attack. Part used is the whole herb.

BROOM
(Cytisus scoparius) Broom is cleansing and purifying. It is used in exorcism, psychic protection, spell-breaking and the prevention of enchantment. Part used are the flowers and tops.

CINQUEFOIL
(Potentilla) Cinquefoil (five finger grass) increases the power and potency of charms and spells. Use the whole plant.

CLOVER (Red)
(Trifolium pratense) Clover is used to enhance charms of good intent. It aids magic. Use the flower heads.

CLOVE
(Eugenia caryophyllata) Protects against negative forces and ill-wishing. Prevents gossip and slander. Protects from psychic attack. Part used is the dried juvenile flower, as bought in any supermarket.

CRANESBILL
(Geranium dissectum) Use for exorcism, charm and spell-breaking and for psychic protection. Part used is the dried rhizome and leaves.

DILL
(Peucedanum graveolens) In the Middle Ages, Dill was used by magicians in their spells and charms against witchcraft. In Drayton's Nymphaedia are the lines 'therewith her vervain and her dill, that hindereth witches of their will.' Dill is traditionally a herb of magic and power. Use the seeds.

DRAGONS BLOOD

(Daemomorops draco) Use in psychic warfare. Protects and defends. Cleanses a difficult or oppressive atmosphere. Part used is the gum resin. N.B. Dragons Blood is extremely expensive but a little goes a long way.

ELDER

(Sambucus nigra) Elder gives protection from witchcraft, drives away evil spirits and wards off attack. Always ask an Elder tree for permission to take her leaves, bark, flowers or berries out of respect for the Elder Tree Mother who lives within the tree. It is important to tell her why you need her bounty also. Part used - everything.

FENNEL

(Foeniculum vulgare) Fennel is employed, together with St. John's Wort as a protection against evil influences and evil spirits. Part used is the seeds.

FRANKINCENSE

(Boswellia thurifera) Frankincense is an extremely effective purifier. Used in incense it will cleanse the home of all negativity. Part used is the gum resin. Frankincense is a base for church incense.

GALANGAL

(Alpinia officinarum) Galangal is used to increase the potency of spells and charms. It is also used in exorcism, psychic protection and to avert ill-wishing. Part used is the root/rhizome.

GARLIC

(Allium sativum) Garlic has long been employed as a protection against evil and enchantment. Burn with Asafoetida to expel unwanted 'beasties'.

GINGER
(Zingiber officinale) Use for psychic protection and in psychic warfare. Cleanses and purifies. Part used is the root.

HYSSOP
(Hyssopus officinalis) Hyssop is used for cleansing sacred places 'purge me with hyssop, and I shall be clean' was written in the scriptures. Removes an oppressive atmosphere. Part used - whole herb.

LILAC
(Syringa vulgaris) Brings peace and tranquillity. Offers protection from psychic attack. Parts used - leaves, flowers and fruit.

LOVAGE
(Levisticum officinale) Protective. Parts used - root, leaves and stems and seeds.

MARJORAM
(Origanum marjorana) Creates an atmosphere of peace and harmony. Protects animals. Part used - whole herb.

MELILOT
(Melilotus officinalis) Brings luck and removes negativity. Protective for animals and humans. Creates strength and courage.

MISTLETOE
(Viscum album) Protects and preserves from all evil.

MUGWORT
(Artemisia vulgaris) Protects and preserves from evil influences and spirits. Protects from attack by wild animals. Used in spell-breaking. Part used - whole herb.

MYRRH
(Commiphora myrrha) Used in fumigation and cleansing. Protects against psychic attack. Used to negate ill-wishing. Part used - gum resin.

NETTLE
(Urtica urens) Used in exorcism, removing enchantments and spell-breaking. Useful in psychic warfare. Part used - whole herb and seeds.

OREGANO
(Origanum vulgare) Brings a calm and peaceful atmosphere. Used in psychic protection. Guards animals. Part used - leaves and stems.

PATCHOULI
(Pogostemon patchouli) Used in exorcism, psychic protection and warfare. Part used - leaves.

PINE NEEDLES
(Pinus) Protective, cleansing and purifying. Use to fight psychic attack and to protect animals.

ROSEMARY
(Rosmarinus officinalis) Purifies, protects and strengthens. A powerful incense herb. Part used - leaves.

RUE
(Ruta graveolens) Rue is an extremely powerful herb for both attack and defence against the powers of magic. 'Rue for regret'. Part used - leaves and stems.

SAGE
(Salvia officinalis) Sage preserves against evil atmospheres and influences. Protects against poisonous thoughts. Part used - leaves.

ST. JOHN'S WORT
(Hypericum perforatum) Used in psychic protection, removing enchantment, magic and exorcism. Part used - leaves and flowers.

SOLOMANS SEAL
(Polygonatum multiflorum) Brings wisdom and clarity to psychic matters. Protective. Used in exorcism and the removal of evil influences. Part used - leaves.

STAR ANISE
(Illicuim verum) Sacred and protective. The tree is planted in Japan around temples and tombs. The bark is burnt as incense. Part used - dried flower casings and seeds.

STORAX
(Liquidambar orientalis) Used in church incense. Purifies and protects. Used in exorcism and spell-breaking. Clears away negativity and the effects of psychic attack. Part used - liquid gum.

VALERIAN
(Valeriana officinalis) Brings peace and harmony. Prevents attack and fighting. Calming. Protects animals. Part used - root.

VERVAIN
(Verbena officinalis) A herb of great magical power. Used in ritual to enhance procedings. Prevents attack through nightmares. Adds potency to charms and spells. Vervain is an ingredient of anointing ointments. Part used - leaves and stems.

WORMWOOD
(Artemisia absinthium) Powerful herb which protects against evil influences. It is said to protect against dragons and wild animals. Guards against psychic attack. Parts used - stems and leaves.

YARROW
(Achillea millefolium) Increases potency and power of charms and spells. Protective. Use in destroying enchantment and ill-wishing. Parts used - leaves and flowers.

INCENSE

Incense is made from a combination of herbs, roots, gums and resins which are combined together and then smouldered on a hot charcoal disc. The resulting perfumed smoke is a very important factor in the effectiveness of ritual and the consecration of talismans, charms and amulets. Incense is of the power of Air.

Incenses should be blended with meticulous care and attention, using ingredients suitable for its intended purpose. It is important to keep a notebook handy for jotting down details of quantity used of each particular herb or resin. It can be most irritating when you wish to make another batch of a good incense, only to find you have forgotten the recipe.

Effective incenses for psychic protection can be formulated from the list of herbs in this chapter. The most successful method includes herbs, roots and resins. A purely herbal incense, though effective, tends to burn away very quickly. Roots are slower burning and resins add perfume in addition to having purification properties.

Try to blend several incenses for different purposes, keeping them in small jars such as empty herb containers or even meat paste jars. Label them carefully. Keep your collection in a place where they are easily accessible. It is no use being under attack in a circle when your incenses are in the kitchen cupboard!

The measure used for incense should be kept for that purpose; it may be a teaspoon or a tablespoon, depending on the quantity required. I use a scoop from a tin of baby milk. Incenses can be blended in a special bowl kept for that purpose or in something as simple as a margarine tub or jam jar. A pestle and mortar is a useful addition which will enable you to grind ingredients down to a suitable size.

RECIPES

PSYCHIC PROTECTION INCENSE:

Burn during circle work.

1	Frankincense
1	Bay Leaves (crushed)
1/2	Star Anise (crushed)
1/2	Cloves (crushed)
1	Basil
1	Vervain
1	Dill Seeds

Blend together, mixing well.

ERADICATION INCENSE:
Burn to repel imps and nasties.

1 Asafoetida
1/4 Garlic (crushed)
1 Myrrh

Use only in the direst necessity. This incense is really foul and the smell lingers for a long time.

INCENSE FOR REFLECTING AN ATTACK TO SOURCE: (and smacking fingers in the process!)

1 Dragons Blood
1 Ginger (powdered or crushed root)
1 Elder (leaves or crushed wood/bark)
1 Rue
1 Valerian
1 Basil
1 Pine Needles (optional)

PROTECTION OF ANIMALS:
Use to bless a protective talisman.

1 Valerian
1 Melilot
1 Mugwort
1 Oregano
1 Frankincense

HOUSE BLESSING INCENSE:

1	Frankincense
1	Myrrh
1	Angelica
1	Agrimony
1	Bay
1	Elder
1/2	Dill Seeds
1	Galangal
1/4	Cinquefoil

Fume property for cleansing and protection in accordance with the House Blessing ritual.

INCENSE FOR THE CONSECRATION OF TALISMANS, AMULETS AND CHARMS:
(for protection)

1	Wormwood
1	Rue
1	Dragons Blood
1	Vervain
1	Frankincense

Fume the talisman in the smoke to bless and consecrate.

CHURCH INCENSE:

4	Frankincense
1	Benzoin
1/4	Storax

Blend together thoroughly. Use as a general purpose incense.

GENERAL ALL PURPOSE INCENSE:

Not a psychic protection incense, but a general working one suitable for most occasions.

1 Frankincense
1 Myrrh
1 Rosemary
1 Soloman's Seal
1 Vervain
1 Mint (any garden mint)

Experiment with different herbs from the list to formulate your own special blends. Trial and error is the only sure way to success. It is incidentally, a good idea to use a tiny measure for testing and experimental purposes.

CENSERS AND THURIBLES

Incense is smouldered on a hot charcoal disc which should be contained within an incense burner (a censer or thurible). These can be obtained from new age suppliers or a brass or fireproof ceramic bowl could be utilised instead. It is a good idea to fill the bowl with sand beforehand to dissipate the heat from the glowing charcoal.

Easy-light charcoal discs are easily available. These should be held in a flame for a few moments until they begin to spark, then allowed to turn white (rather like barbeque charcoal) before sprinkling the blended incense on the top.

Use incense very sparingly - a little goes a long way.

THE PROTECTIVE GARDEN

Trees which have white blossom and red berries are protective against the evil-eye, 'bad fairies' and witchcraft. Rowan, hawthorn, holly and elder all fall into this category. A garden hedge made up of, or including these trees will preserve the home and garden from dark influences.

HOLLY

Holly has sharp, prickly, shiny leaves and no animal will graze upon it. Its prickly leaves and scarlet berries are offensive to evil spirits. Holly should never be pruned needlessly but should be left to spread and mature to enable it to protect the home. Holly is often planted near the house door as a protective measure. A holly that is self sown should never be moved to another location as it has chosen to grow in the place most suited to its protective influence.

ROWAN

The name 'rowan' comes from the Swedish 'r n' which is derived from 'rune' giving the rowan the title of 'magic tree'. Twigs and switches of rowan have been accepted as a protection against magic for a long time. A rowan in the garden, or planted near a door is a time-honoured protective force against evil and witchcraft.

ELDER

Elder protects the house and garden from sorcery and evil influences. The berries are a protection against malevolence. It is considered very unlucky to cut or prune an elder without asking the permission of the Elder Tree Mother, who lives in the tree, beforehand. If cutting is unavoidable the following rhyme should be recited:

> 'Lady Elder, give me thy wood,
> And I will give thee of mine,
> When I become a tree!'

An elder hedge affords great protection from evil spirits and dark forces. Elders can grow from seemingly dead sticks. I once bought a climbing hydrangea for my kitchen wall and supported it with an elder stick which had been lying at the top of the garden for months. The hydrangea curled up its roots and died, and yes, the elder stick grew into a lovely tree.

HAWTHORN

Hawthorns should be allowed to grow where they strike. It is unlucky to move a hawthorn from its chosen place in the garden. An old saying relates, 'Hawthorn amongst the hedging plants will ward off bad fairies.' I once moved a small hawthorn to another location in my garden. It did not thrive, but became very sick indeed, even to its leaves turning white with a powdery substance. I moved it back to its original site and it is now thriving.

Other protective garden plants are: Ivy - which acts a protective guardian as it climbs up a house wall. Lilac and Honeysuckle prevent evil spirits from entering property. Rosemary disperses evil influences and Oregano and Snapdragons (Antirrnums) break spells and charms.

In my own garden I have all the above-mentioned plants and trees, some were planted but most of them have just appeared there and flourished.

It is a good idea to cultivate a herb garden, both for culinary purposes and for supplying yourself with herbs that are necessary for incense making. Home-grown herbs seem to make a better incense than shop bought ones. This is, I believe, because home-grown herbs have flourished in a caring environment, they have been fed and watered and gathered with loving intent before being carefully dried and stored for use. Herb plants are easily available from specialist nurseries. In my own garden I grow many herbs, including, sage, rosemary, lavender, oregano, thyme, woad, basil, vervain, valerian, wormwood, tansy, comfrey, woodruff, betony, cranesbill and mint to name but a few. It is well worth the time and effort involved in preparing your own herbs for magical use.

HERBAL CHARM FOR PSYCHIC PROTECTION

Cut a circle of red cloth, about six inches in diameter and a length of red cord for tying it up.

Take seven different herbs of protection (from the list). I have chosen, as an example: Frankincense, Basil, Bay Leaves, Hyssop, Vervain, Rue and St. John's Wort. Place the herbs in a dish and blend them together with your fingers, saying:

> Seven herbs of power
> Seven herbs of might
> Guard me from the goblin
> From elves and darkest night.

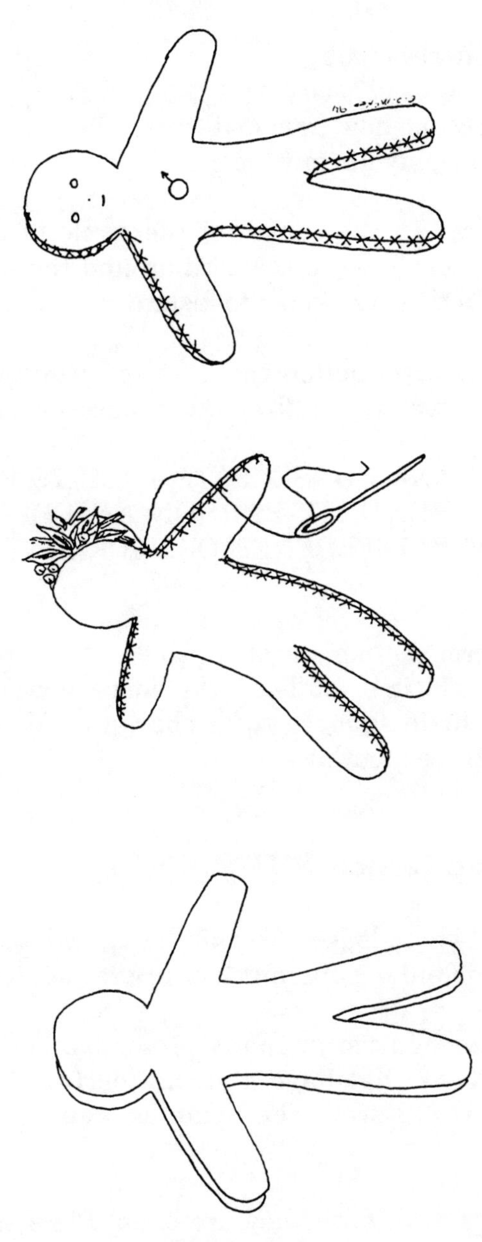

Doll or Poppet

Seven herbs of magic
Seven herbs of good
Preserve me now from evil
My home, my life, my blood.

Place the herbs in the centre of the circle of cloth and gather into a pouch, wrap the cord around the neck three times and then tie three knots to fasten.

Seal the knots with melted candle wax. Now consecrate the charm with water, salt, fire and incense smoke, saying:

I BLESS AND CONSECRATE THEE TO PROTECT AND DEFEND MY PERSON AND PROPERTY FROM THE INFLUENCE OF WICKEDNESS. LET IT BE!

Hang the charm up in a suitable place, such as beside the front door. Each time you leave the house or pass by, give the charm a little squeeze to re-charge it. Make a new charm every three months.

PROTECTIVE GREEN POT-POURRI

Try to collect whole leaves for this herbal mixture as the ground herbs found in supermarkets are rather powdery.

Gather the leaves from as many protective herbs as are available. Those that have a strong perfume are most useful as they will scent the home as well as affording protection.

Dry the leaves well, until they are crisp. Place the mixed leaves in a large polythene bag or an ice-cream container. Add to the leaves 3 tablespoons of orris root powder and 3 drops of lemon oil, lavender oil and rosemary oil. Seal the bag or container, shake well and leave for about six weeks, shaking well every couple of days.

When the pot-pourri has matured bless and consecrate it as for the Herbal Charm and then divide it between several bowls and place them around the house. Riffle your fingers through the pot pourri periodically to re-charge it.

DOLL MAGIC

If you know you are under a psychic attack from a particular person (you must be absolutely certain) it is possible to protect yourself by making an image doll or poppet.

Cut out a pattern (as shown in the diagram) from red felt or cloth, red being a protective colour and under the rulership of Mars (the planet of the warrior). Hand-sew the doll together, leaving a gap at the top of the head to allow filling. Choose a selection of protective herbs from the list, nine in all, that being the number of Mars. Mix the herbs together, then stuff the sewn doll with the herbs. Sew up the opening. Draw, paint or embroider the symbol of Mars on the front of the chest. Then draw a face on the doll's head. The symbol of Mars is:

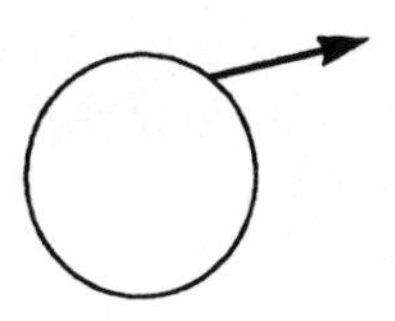

Bless and consecrate the doll, with water, salt, fire and incense smoke, and then name it for the person who wishes you harm, saying:

> 'THIS IS _______name_______. HE LIVES AND BREATHES, HE IS ALIVE!'

Visualise the doll as taking on the persona of the person who wishes you harm.

> '_______name________ YOU CANNOT HARM ME, YOUR POWER IS NOTHING. I TIE YOUR HANDS. I SEAL YOUR LIPS.

(Bind the doll's hands together with thread and sew up it's mouth).

> YOU CAN DO NO EVIL AND YOU CAN SPEAK NO EVIL. YOUR INFLUENCE IS GONE.

Hold the doll in your hands and feel the influence of your attacker leaving you. Wrap the doll up in a piece of clean cloth and put it away somewhere safe and secure. You may keep the doll for a year and a day. After that time has elapsed you should carefully unbind it and take it apart in reverse order to it's making. Burn or bury the remains. Do not burn or bury the doll whole!

Think carefully before you undertake any kind of image magic. I cannot stress too strongly the importance of being absolutely sure you are under attack.

CHAPTER 13

RITES AND RITUALS

HOUSE BLESSING RITUAL

Before beginning this ritual it is important to take a bath or shower to purify and cleanse the person. Prepare your circle or the room you have chosen to work in. Draw your circle in your usual manner or perform the opening ritual given in Chapter 3. Have ready on your altar a dish of salt, a dish of water, some incense and a red candle. Bless and purify these as follows:

Water: Draw a banishing pentacle through the water with your forefinger and say:

I CLEANSE AND PURIFY THEE
O BEING OF WATER
LET ALL UNWHOLESOMENESS
AND POLLUTION BE GONE FROM THEE
AND LET VIRTUE LIVE WITHIN THEE.

Salt: Draw an invoking pentacle of earth through the salt and say:

GRACE BE WITHIN THIS BEING OF EARTH
LET ALL THAT IS BANEFUL BE GONE FROM THEE
AND LET ALL THAT IS FAVOURABLE
BE BORN WITHIN THEE
I CONJURE THEE, O POWER OF EARTH
TO ASSIST AND AID ME.

Pour the salt into the water and stir together in a sunwise spiral direction.

Incense: Sprinkle some incense onto the hot charcoal and say:

BEING OF AIR I CHARGE THEE
LET ALL THAT IS UNCLEAN BE GONE FROM THEE
LET PURITY RISE IN THY PERFUME
AID ME IN MY WORK!

Candle: Light the red candle and say:

POWER BE IN THIS CREATURE OF FIRE
MAY ALL THAT IS GOOD BURN WITHIN THEE
AND MAY ALL THAT IS PREJUDICE BURN OUT
AID ME IN MY WORK!

Gather the salt water, the censer and the candle together, open the circle with a sweep of the hand, leave it and quickly close it behind you with three sweeps of the hand. Take each element outside and one by one and cleanse and purify (by sprinkling the salt water on the ground), cense and light the outside walls of your house. Then repeat at the outer perimeters of your property.

When this is completed go back indoors and repeat inside, paying special attention to doors and windows by following the frames all round. When all is completed return to your circle, opening and closing it carefully as you proceed.

Stand in the East and say:

> I INVOKE THE POWERS OF AIR FOR THE BLESSING OF THIS HOME (AND TEMPLE). BY THE POWERS OF GOOD, I ASK FOR YOUR

PROTECTION OF THIS PLACE. LET NO EVIL ENTER HERE. LET YOUR INFLUENCE OF AIR GRANT US INTELLIGENCE AND CLARITY OF THOUGHT. LET YOUR QUICK FINGERS WEAVE AROUND THIS PLACE A WEB OF PEACE. BY THE MIGHT OF THE SUN AT DAWN, WRAP YOUR PROTECTION OVER US AND LET US GROW IN PEACE, PROSPERITY AND HEALTH.

Concentrate for a while and visualise a cleansing wind blowing all hindrance away.

Stand in the South and say:

I INVOKE THE POWERS OF FIRE FOR THE BLESSING OF THIS HOME (AND TEMPLE). BY THE POWERS OF GOOD I ASK FOR YOUR PROTECTION IN THIS PLACE. LET NO EVIL ENTER HERE. LET THE INFLUENCE OF FIRE GRANT US STRENGTH, COURAGE AND ENERGY AND LAY AROUND THIS PLACE THE FIRES OF KNOWLEDGE AND UNDERSTANDING. BY THE MIGHT OF THE SUN AT NOON, PLACE YOUR PROTECTION OVER US AND LET US GROW IN PEACE, PROSPERITY AND HEALTH.

Concentrate for a while and visualise a friendly and comforting warmth filling the house.

Stand in the West and say:

I INVOKE THE POWERS OF WATER FOR THE BLESSING OF THIS HOME (AND TEMPLE). BY THE POWER OF GOOD, I ASK FOR YOUR PROTECTION IN THIS PLACE. LET NO EVIL ENTER HERE. LET THE INFLUENCE OF WATER

GRANT US VISION AND EMOTIONAL PURITY, LEND US YOUR POWERS OF LOVE AND UNDERSTANDING. LET YOUR SOOTHING WATERS WASH AWAY ALL SADNESS AND PAIN. BY THE MIGHT OF THE SUN AT DUSK, PLACE YOUR PROTECTION OVER US AND LET US GROW IN PEACE, PROSPERITY AND HEALTH.

Concentrate for a while and visualise a gentle shower of refreshing rain pouring over you.

Stand in the North and say:

I INVOKE THE POWERS OF EARTH FOR THE BLESSING OF THIS HOME (AND TEMPLE). BY THE POWERS OF GOOD WE ASK FOR YOUR PROTECTION IN THIS PLACE. LET NO EVIL ENTER HERE. LET THE INFLUENCE OF EARTH GRANT US STEADFASTNESS, PATIENCE, STABILITY AND WILLPOWER AND LAY ABOUT THIS PLACE THE STONES OF ENDURANCE. BY THE MIGHT OF THE SUN AT MIDNIGHT, PLACE YOUR PROTECTION OVER US AND LET US GROW IN PEACE, PROSPERITY AND HEALTH.

Concentrate for a while and visualise the firm solidity of the earth protecting the house.

Look upwards and say:

SPIRITS ABOVE GRANT US YOUR PROTECTION.

Look down and say:

SPIRITS BELOW GRANT US YOUR PROTECTION.

Visualise electric blue light in your solar plexus area and then gradually push it outwards to the boundaries of your property, cleansing and securing everything it touches.

Close the circle now if you wish; or continue by preparing and consecrating seals and talismans of protection. When completed, the seals are placed at the farthest points, east, south, west and north of your property. This may be either in the home, the garden boundaries or both.

SEALS OF PROTECTION

Seals of protection incorporate a factor from each of the four elements, i.e:

air = a feather or mercury

fire = sulphur or saltpetre

water = water

earth = salt or clean soil.

To prepare your seals you will need four small bottles or jars. Fill the bottles with a portion of each element. Bless and consecrate them by saying:

I BLESS THEE AND PURIFY THEE

(draw a banishing pentacle over each bottle)

BEINGS OF AIR, FIRE, WATER AND EARTH. I CHARGE THEE TO BE A PROTECTION AND A GUARD AGAINST ALL EVIL WHICH WOULD TRY TO ENTER HERE

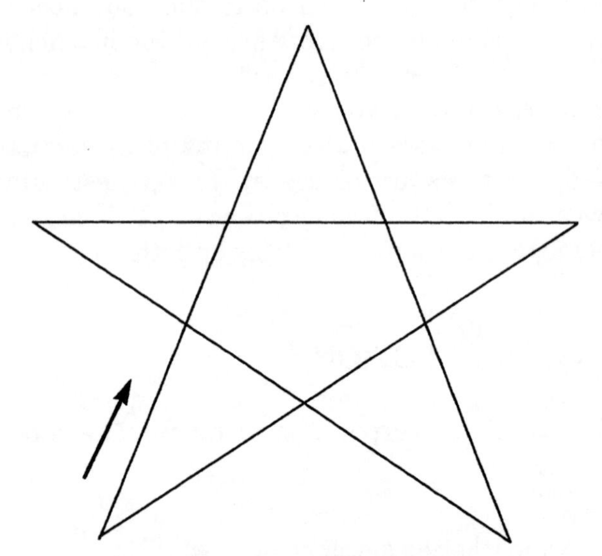

Banishing Pentacle of Earth

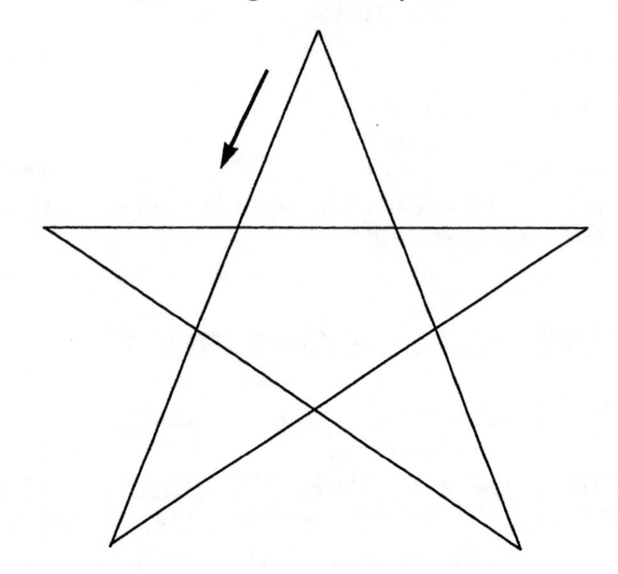

Invoking Pentacle of Earth

(draw an invoking pentacle over each bottle)

LET IT BE!

You may also wish to add a talisman to each bottle i.e. a talisman for air, one for fire, one for water and one for earth. When you have added your talisman make sure you know which bottle is which. Mark each bottle if necessary. It would be difficult, for instance, for an air talisman to work effectively if you placed it in the west. Close each bottle tightly and then seal the lids with the wax from a red candle.

TALISMANS

To make your elemental talismans, draw a suitable picture on one side which relates to its intended element; e.g. a chalice for water, a feather or sword for air, etc. On the other side write a simple phrase such as, PROTECT THIS PLACE FROM EVIL, NOTHING SHALL ENTER HERE. Then bless and empower it as detailed in Chapter 9.

PROTECTION OF ANIMALS

Animals are very susceptible to the effects of psychic attack and are unable to protect themselves against such influences. The House Blessing Ritual gives protection to all people and creatures which live in the house, but many animals, cats especially, often wander away from the boundaries and therefore are left open to unpleasant encounters.

A pet is a well-loved member of the family. If the pet suffers then so do its owners. What better method could someone with ill-intent use to hurt you.

Small metal cylinders which screw together in the middle can be purchased from any pet shop. These are intended to fit onto a collar and hold a slip of paper with the animal's name and address written on it. They can also be used to contain a protective talisman.

Make the talisman as detailed in Chapter 9, using your imagination to create a picture suitable for your pet. Include the pet's name in the wording on the other side, e.g. THIS GUARDS CREIRWY FROM HARM BOTH SEEN AND UNSEEN. Bless and consecrate the talisman and attach to the pet's collar.

THE BANISHING PENTACLE

The drawing of a Banishing Pentacle in the air in front of you will clear almost any manifestation or entity. The Pentacle is a symbol of immense power and is a very effective weapon against psychic attack.

Draw a banishing pentacle as large as possible using the forefinger of your dominant hand. The arm should be held straight in front of you. Draw your pentacle as if you mean it, with magical intent.

Begin at a point level with your left hip, then draw a line with your finger to a point above the centre of your head, draw a line from there, down to your right hip, then up again to a point level with your left shoulder, then across to your right shoulder and then down again to your left hip. The Pentacle should be drawn in a smooth, flowing manner. Lastly stab the centre of your pentacle with your forefinger to empower it.

One Samhain (Hallowe'en) one of my sons had bought a toy, glow-in-the-dark, shrunken head with long, flowing hair attached. Our cats were very interested in this, so I hung it up from a hook on the ceiling in the dining room, to keep it out of their way. We did our Samhain working and after we had finished, a person who shall be nameless, walked into the dining room without switching on the light and saw a disembodied head floating in the air above him. He immediately drew a banishing pentacle at it, to no effect. He forthwith, did what all good Wiccans do - he ran away to get reinforcements. 'He who shall be nameless' has still not lived it down!

CHAPTER 14

INTERVIEWS AND EXPERIENCES

I interviewed a number of friends and acquaintances from various parts of Britain and Ireland, who have differing spiritual beliefs, and asked them what methods of psychic self-defence they utilised in protecting themselves, their homes and their families. I also asked them to talk about any experiences of psychic attack they had come across and how they had coped with it.

Interview with Jane from Cardiff

"The first psychic attack that I noticed was soon after we started to become active in the craft. It was really just after I met Thomas. We were with a couple of friends who were also interested in psychic stuff. I had actually read a book on Wicca at this stage (good old Raymond Buckland) and we actually went into a psychic shop in the Midlands. It was as though this chap there ... the shop was a bit dodgy, he had a few skulls and candles around and things like that, making a show, there was a robe with an upside down pentagram on it. I think this person had the initials C.M.

I was quite young and he absolutely took a shine to me. It was just like this tremendous energy that went into me, like a focus lamp on me. I was just totally bewildered by the light. It was like someone paying incredible attention to me. He said something like, 'I like what I see, and I'll have it' or something like that. Thomas and Dave just felt as though he had dropped a bucket of cold water on them both and Jenny was in the background frightened. This was done without saying anything. It was as though he saw the two men there protecting me and dropped this psychic bucket of cold water on them. We all scooted out of the shop and we were quite frightened by this. It was quite a tremendous psychic experience.

After that there were a few psychic mishaps that happened to people, Dave broke his leg. Thomas and I were lying down together once and I felt what was almost like chewing gum fibres between us and I felt like I was being pulled away. It was really difficult, almost like he was trying to break the love between me and Thomas. We got rid of it over time. It think it was mainly our love and the group staying together. The temptation and this energy was telling me 'You are going to come back here, and you're going to be mine.' We all resisted the temptation to ever go back there again. We still haven't.

When we first found the Craft we read the books which told you how to set up a circle, but they didn't tell you what to do when you had set up the circle. We were very naive at the time, and there we were on the nineteenth floor of a tower block in Birmingham. We set down a circle and it was really nice, we had beautiful music playing. We had just met each other and were very much in love, so we made love in the circle, which is a pretty good way to raise power (laughter).

Suddenly I just looked at Thomas and I saw his aura and it was black and it was green and changing into this demon face. We immediately shut down the circle, and he was trying to calm me down, because I just didn't believe it was him. He suddenly said that my entire face and my body changed into that of a very, very young girl. I stayed like that for about five minutes, really, really young then suddenly went really, really old. We got rid of that by shutting down the circle and holding each other. It was a pretty silly thing to do really.

The biggest thing that was fairly recent was the one with Jamie. I suddenly had this dream, it was one of my very active dreams where I was trying to get in to my son Jamie and there was this icy wind that was blowing, and a force was holding me back. I really fought against the force to get into Jamie's bedroom, grabbed Jamie and tried to get out with him.

When we got outside the door I realised that I wasn't really holding Jamie, it was as though I had been dummied by something. So I went back in and did a banishing pentagram. It was really the force of my own will that got me back in there. I grabbed Jamie and got out of the room with him. Thomas sensed the same sort of thing but in a different form. He will tell you about that. I think Jamie realised that something was trying to take a nibble at him because there was a mirror in his cot and he actually managed to turn it round. Even though he was so young, he wasn't able to use his hands at all.

There have been loads of times when I have thought I was under psychic attack from psychic vampirism and what I do when that happens and I start to feel drained, is just bolster up my own aura and sphere of light. I can put mirrors on the outside. I imagine from the psychic vampire a tentacle coming from their aura to my aura, that is where it is sucking all my energy from. And then what I do is hold a sword of light in one hand and a torch of fire in the other hand. I swipe and cut the tentacle with the sword and then I cauterize it with the torch to seal it in without harming the person.

I use psychic protection for physical threats. At one time the local mafia were trying to damage Thomas; it was something to do with his car. It was a threat. The entire coven did a protection ritual. They also had a talisman and one of the girls put it on her altar. We had no problems from the mafia at all. About a year later she was clearing out her altar and took off the talisman to protect Thomas's car and immediately it broke down. I had to tell her to put it back on the altar again.

We have been under psychic attack as a coven, where people were ill, animals were ill and eight people had their crystals broken on the same day. It just affected everybody, the minor members of the coven as well.

You could mention about the house protections as well. We put seals on the house. I have got two crouching Anubis statues in the cupboards downstairs, and each one has a stone that is taken from a Temple Shrine of Anubis in Egypt. There are two of them from two different shrines. When John tried to come into our house (astrally, to help clear the problem with Jamie, he came across this twenty foot Anubis. Strangely enough, we were at one time doing some work with M & J, trying to get into each others houses and M said, without knowing what John had said, that he came across exactly the same thing. That worked and that was without even asking Anubis for protection. I got into M & J's without any problem, they have got mirrored panels all over their bedroom and the mirrors hadn't been sealed, so it was easy.

We used to move from a lot of rented accommodation and we have a stone, which we call our dragon's egg. We put the essence of the house (because I think the house forms an entity of itself), and we actually put the entity of the house into the stone. It is the last thing that leaves, and as we come into the new house then we release it and have the entity in the new house. The dragon egg lives in the airing cupboard.

I have had to defend myself when I have been in hospital. I have found that when I go under, especially when I was on Pethidine, I was just wandering the hospital aimlessly. I was walking on the ceilings, I went into the kitchens and it was just awful. What I had to do, before I went for the operation was make the sphere of light like a sarcophagus, with different layers and I had seals on the outside.

If I am under physical threat, like when I am on my own or with another member of staff in the pharmacy, I could easily get attacked. I have people who come into the shop who are threatening. I actually have Anubis standing just behind me and he puts his head there (on top of my head) or two really big black dogs appear on either side of me, and they can stay there or stand at the entrance of the shop. Once this person has left they will not come back in again. I have never known anyone to come back in again.

There was one time when there was a child who was under psychic attack, it was some friends of ours who asked us to come in. There was a group of us working together. I can't remember how the situation arose, anyway it just suddenly happened with me that I worked with one of my past selves to work with this particular problem. Part of me believes that I had a past life in Egypt, and that I was a High Priestess. I have worked with her before, as it were, I danced through her, things like that.

My stipulation is that as far as my personal defence goes when working with her that she is a distinct entity away from me in certain ways, so that when I work with her, I will actually go to her, I will not let her come to me, so she can't invade my space. If she is happy with me working in her circle then that is fine, she could always tell me to go. I think she works with Sekhmet. We had Anubis, me and me in a past life working together to solve this girl's problem. There we set her up with a sarcophagus protection, she just needed a static protection, and it seemed to work. When we left the circle some friends who were into Egyptian stuff knew precisely what we had been up to. It was something different to work with my past life.

When I worked in a London hospital, downstairs was where all the people injured in the war would have gone. There was an awful lot of suffering. The whole hospital had a really bad atmosphere. Because I had been doing the sphere of light so much, I would actually be walking down to the pharmacy department and suddenly realise that my sphere of light was up. I would think, 'What the hell is happening?' and then I would sense a figure going past, or something. It was almost like I had set up Hermetic warning signals and my defences had gone up straight away.

We have got the 'chaos crystal'. You have to be very careful what you do. We just have it in a little silk pouch, put away. If you wear it, dramatic changes happen in your life. This thing wriggles out of clasps and things like that. It does not want to be worn. We make sure it is bound up carefully and not touched. If someone is in a dead relationship and needs a change, we give it to them. It always comes back to us. It serves a purpose but it is awful."

Interview with Thomas from Cardiff

"The first time we bumped up against someone, I am sure Jane's told this story anyway, I wouldn't call it an attack exactly, but more poking fun, it was ... Jane and I had discovered Raymond Buckland's book and we were all into this. We wimbled along with a couple of friends who knew even less, they thought we were some kind of gurus, and we wimbled into this psychic bookshop in the Midlands, which I believe is now gone. The owner of the shop was called C.M. I was so frightened by this afterwards that I actually deleted his name from my memory, using a little trick that I picked up, and only left the initials, so I could never remember who he was. I could probably get it if I wanted to, but I am quite content to leave it at that.

We went into the shop and he took a shine to Jane and the first that the rest of us knew about it was the pressure of this will that just rolled over you. He was talking to Jane and the rest of us were just squirrelled away into little pockets of 'this can't be happening'. It was like being frozen with fright. We were just trying to pretend that nothing was happening. His voice was in the background talking to Jane and she was just standing there with her mouth open. We didn't know what the hell was going on. What he said to her was, 'You'd better not come back into this shop because if you come back, I'm going to decide that I want you and will never let you leave'. It lifted after a while and I just grabbed everybody and threw them all out of the shop and got away.

Jane wasn't right for days. She was trying to hug inside my aura all the time, because she felt less of a pull. She thought there was a definite pull for her to go back to this guy in the Midlands. It frightened the hell out of us. All it was was this guy's will, all he did really was to throw a portion of himself at her and to blanket us. We had absolutely no defence against him. We had never heard of such a thing. Psychic attack... the only thing we knew was out of 'The Devil Rides Out'.

My ideas of protection in those days entailed probably slaughtering a goat, drawing some very dodgy sigils on the ground and having some huge candlesticks. So I think really that anybody starting out needs to know how to assert. Dabbling is dangerous. The very first thing I have taught all my own students since, is how to defend themselves. Before they know what else they can do, they are defending themselves.

The most useful method of psychic self-defence that I have encountered is the *Sphere of Light*, which is an auric reinforcement. I used to use a version called the *Tower of Light*, and that was consisting of imagining a nice picture of your own aura as being a nice contained tube in which you are standing. You imagine this ball of light appearing above you at the crown chakra, then golden rain coming down, clearing everything out, and that worked fairly well.

If I can remember back to that time, having not experienced a lot of auric work, I was very impressed with how clear-headed this made me feel. But since then I now use one known as the *Sphere of Light*. You start off in your solar plexus, with a point of light of whatever colour... blue grey tends to be my standard colour which is the way that I perceive untuned energy. I start with that and then I draw energy in and make it bigger and bigger until I am standing inside it, rather than it being inside of me.

The *Sphere of Light* not only works if I perceive that there is any negative energy on me ... it also works for pain. If I have got tension in my shoulders, I see that as a different coloured energy, and when it passes through that it sweeps it out and goes with the edge of it. If necessary, I will do another couple of these that merge into the one that pre-exists. It can be tuned different ways. If I am getting the 'evil-eye' or something, I can mirror it and send it back and so on. It works nicely. Or I can be invisible by wearing a dark purple colour that is psychically invisible. If you are walking to or from the train station last thing at night and you see some yobboes coming the other way, you put your head down, in some way this seems to make your aura stronger, put your arms in front of you, and walk purposefully as if you know where you are going.

The other *Sphere of Light* where you tie an action in with a complex magical operation. Oh, yes, Hermetics. You always do the action when you do the magical operation, until just doing the action causes the operation to happen. You link the *Sphere of Light* with an action and in my case, I just hum and the *Sphere* goes up.

After a while the *Sphere of Light* began to go up without provocation and I knew I was in trouble. I would think, 'Oh, my *Sphere of Light*'s gone up. What's caused that?' If I had been doing this actively, when I went to that shop in the Midlands, I wouldn't have perceived that anything was happening at all. I would have wondered why my sphere went up, taken a good look at the chap and got the hell out. When we first went in there I was so open... begging someone to recognise me, or see my aura or something.

I am sure that Jane has told you about the Jamie episode. I saw it in an entirely different way. I had a dream as well, but I preceived the whole thing in different terms. In my dream there was something wrong. I can't remember what it was that drew me into the room, but there was something there. The door was cold to the touch ... I

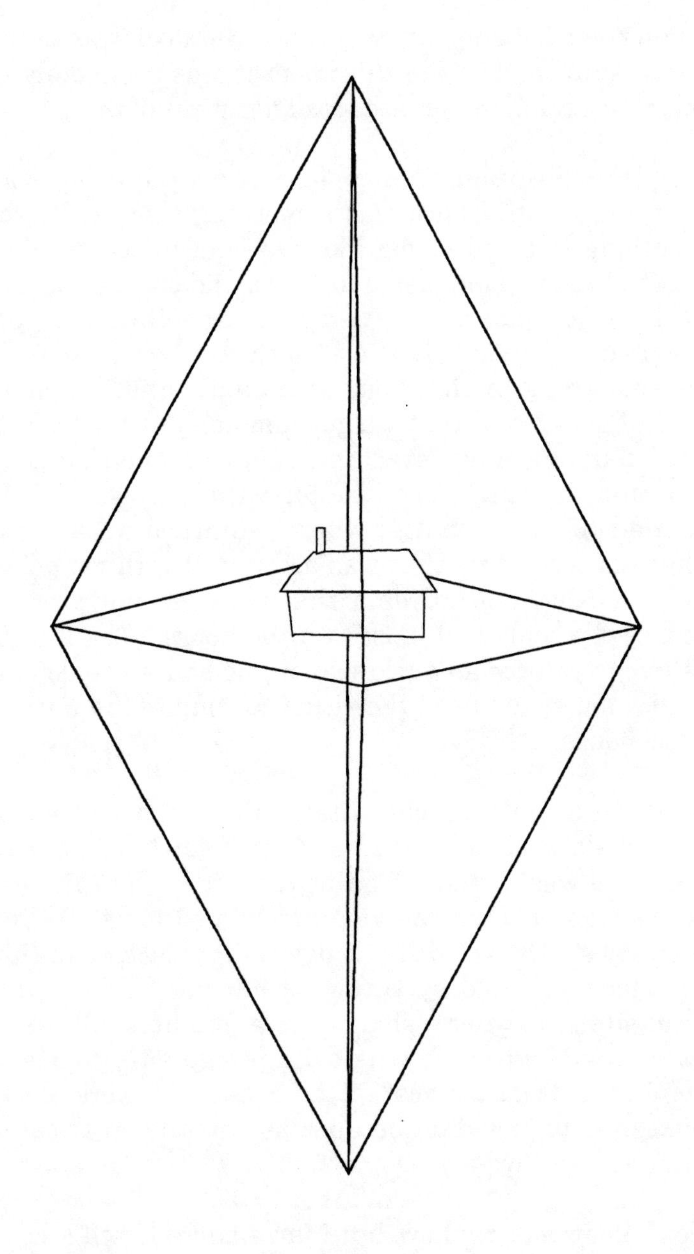

couldn't get it open. It was frost; the door was actually frosted shut, and inside this room it was completely dark and icy, icy cold. My breath was falling out of the air.

I got into the room and picked him up and he wasn't breathing at all. There was something else in the room. Something tall and black, like the man in the Sandeman advert. I held Jamie inside my aura and opened his mouth and breathed into him. Then I got myself out. It was a very peculiar dream. Jane an I both got the idea that there was something in the room with Jamie and that his life was in danger, and that we got him out. At that point we contacted you, and Peter and every damned person we knew and went right over the top with Anubis. Now I am inclined to think that it wasn't so much an attack on Jamie, as something that was associated with us, pointing out to us through a dream that we were not protected, because the seals had lapsed on the house. The danger is that when you see an auric seal on the house you don't do a ritual. You really need the ritual to solidify the auric seal on the house.

There was a run of psychic attacks that happened when we were at Maria's. There was a chap, I can't remember his name - he was in the media at the time, about five years ago, he was another one who proclaimed himself 'King of all Witches'. He was doing dodgy things, such as initiating a fourteen year old by throwing her naked down into a burial site somewhere, along with a human skull. And as always, with that, it was a huge ego thing. He was vampirising from the rest of the coven who were allowing themselves to be fed off because he was the great satanist guru etc.

I don't know exactly how, but Maria had allowed a book to get out of her hands. It was a very old book containing some summoning rituals and it had got to this chap and he had refused to return it. One of his group, who had fallen out of favour managed to get into his house, stole the book and performed one of the summoning rituals. It was some Russian demons that this ritual was to summon, known collectively as The Howling or the Howling Demons, and these damned things weren't aimed at all. For some reason they decided to go back to the owner of the book, which happened to be Maria. Maria's house was fairly well sealed at the time and all the rest of us had house sealings of various shapes and size, so the effects came down to the relatives and pets and cars because there is only so much protection you can do.

This demon thing happened at the same time as the Zeebrugge ferry disaster, there was a suggestion that that may also have been a result of the summoning ritual. Apparently it was a doozie. All the disasters that happened, happened to the family of those that did the summoning ritual, so it must have somehow rebounded. Nothing actually happened to the girl who performed the summoning as far as I know.

Sphere of Light - Visualise a ball of light in the solar plexus and expand it until it is just big enough to contain the individual member of the group, then expand the sphere until the group merges into a coherent whole. Once firmly visualised it will hold for thirty to sixty minutes and should be repeated half-hourly as necessary with modification, because once you have done it you don't need to keep your attention on it. It will just hold like a bubble.

If you are feeling tired and drained, assume the closed position, which is crossing the arms, closing the legs together and putting the head down. If you meet a psychic vampire on the astral who tries to drain you, you can see the link as an actual tentacle, coloured a sick green. Visualise yourself with a sword cutting the link in half, then cauterize with a flaming torch. This actually works and produces a lot of shock in the person who has been draining you as well. You owe this to them - draining is unhealthy - if you shock them then they'll seek higher sources of energy, which is better for them.

Generally if you meet a nasty entity, you tell it to 'bugger off or there will be trouble' that usually does it. Learn your basic protections, the Sphere of Light etc. If you feel you may be in trouble, put your defences up before you need them, and be ready. Stay balanced physically and spiritually.

To seal the house: You have got a picture of the house, with the protection symbols of your choice for each of the six directions; up, down, North, East, South, West. You draw the symbols on pieces of paper, which you put on the highest, lowest, most eastern, most southern, most western and most northern ports. You nail them on or put them under the wallpaper, under the carpet, in the loft etc. You do this lovely picture which is like a diamond in three planes, with the house in the middle, and at each point of the diamond the respective symbol. You put this original picture where you can see it, say half way up the stairs, where each time you see it, you are reminded of the seal of the house and thereby reinforce it.

Interview with John from Shrewsbury

To protect myself, I put a blue light all over me. I am comfortable with blue, some people use white. The light is like a neon blue and acts as if it is electrified. A neon light - very strong. There are no gaps or holes in it and it is very comfortable. The light is charged all the time from above, rather like a spotlight of the same colour. It is a continual thing. It goes down to ground level like a bell-jar and is adequate for my needs. If anything came from underneath, I feel strongly that the light would annihilate it. Nothing will get through it, and once the sealing is done there is no need to worry for the rest of the day. I do this every day. If I am travelling in a vehicle I will do it, but I don't only do it for myself in the vehicle, I tend to cover everybody. Even if the vehicle is moving I visualise the bell jar going over the vehicle and being charged. So in addition to myself being protected, I am protecting the vehicle and everybody in it.

When astrally projecting I do not have a cord attached to me. There are no limitations whatsoever. I know the stories about how people cannot cross water or can't do this or can't do that. There is no cord there and I can travel wherever I please. The astral level appears to be like plasticine, it can be moulded. If there is anything nasty there, my visualisation prefers to see Donald Duck or something like that, so if I am challenged, and it is Donald Duck it is easier to cope with.

I don't change everything of course, but it is possible to alter things on that level. In a sense that if somebody was having a go at me ... you have heard about the Law of Challenge? Well, I challenge the idea of 'you must stop doing this' on the Astral realms. If I see someone sitting there on the astral realms, and this person is having a go at me, I wouldn't challenge him in an occult sense. My first reaction would be to go up and give him a good shaking. He would go back to his physical body very, very quickly, feeling sick and shaken and would think twice about repeating it again.

With certain esoteric workings you can attract, and sometimes you attract waste and garbage. This is why you don't leave your robes out, because like a magnet they attract all sorts of things. An esoteric working can attract garbage, what some people refer to as astral barnacles. If you try to get rid of them, their general reaction is 'Why should I go?' They can be shaken off. Often someone else with knowledge in such a situation can be helpful. I would say that problem is very rare. So nobody should assume that because I work in esoteric fields with other people, that these particular astral barancles will be attracted.

Sometimes one can attract garbage which can be got rid of with cleansing, ritual baths etc. and the realignment of the aura. Most people are unaware of the presence of one. There is an expression, 'monkey on your back'. It manifests in aggression and seems to feed off that aggression. What I have found, over a period of time with anything occult or esoteric, is that people who would instigate a psychic attack are very naive, so as soon as they attack, you are aware immediately. The others would tend to work at the foundations of the building, you wouldn't realise the foundations were gone until the building crumbled.

Interview with Bill from Blythe

What do I do to protect myself? I know what Jayne does; she uses gold light or sometimes blue light to surround the flat, then she does the bed, then she does the car, and the babies, not necessarily in that order. Then she protects the cat. My view to protection ... I'm an arrogant git really, I don't do a lot because my view is that there is nobody out there who can do a lot to me anyway. I tend to ignore it; that is the best way of describing my own protection ... I am not fussed about anything.

In an attacking situation on the astral, well, every night I dream lucid dreams, and if I do have a bogeyman appear to me, it dosn't bother me in the slightest. I just let it carry on regardless. I have this uncanny knack of being able to control dreams. If something is chasing me ... (interruption by child) Anyone, initiates or non-initiates can control their dreams, with training or even without training. So if I feel something is getting a little bit hairy I will steer it in another direction. I have been known to let it go its natural course anyway.

It is common knowledge now, that when you are dreaming you are in the astral realm anyway. I read somwhere that if you die on the astral you die in real life. If that was the case I shouldn't be here at all. I have been stabbed, shot, cut to pieces, beheaded, burnt, drowned, eaten. You name it - it's happened. And I'm still here; not drained of energy in the slightest.

Psychic Vampires - if they want to feed off my energy, it's entirely their own thing. It is up to them. I am not interested enough to worry about it, I am not really affected. Attacks ... if there was somebody out there who was to light a candle, say, to have a go, the only effect Jayne and I would notice would be a splash-on effect. If we have had an attack, then it has been so weak and undirected that it just hasn't affected us. We tend to find that we feed off each other, which is a protection in itself. What I mean by that is ... there was a situation a few weeks ago; I figured out, with the nameless one ... the woman, and it was manifesting itself with aggression more than anything. I was feeling aggressive to anything around me and everybody around me and likewise with other people. But apart from that, it wasn't really anything to write home about. It was very, very quickly found, and very, very quickly stopped; more or less instantaneously.

I have always viewed it, that if there is somebody out there who actually knows what they are doing, I would know sod all about it until it was too late anyway. It would start from the bottom and work upwards, not the other way round. If I was going to attack somebody, I would not jump out in front of them and say, 'Hello. I'm going to attack you.' I would creep up behind them and knock them on the back of the head. That is the best way to describe it.

As for attacking other people, well that's a whole new ball game. I get a buzz out of being wicked. Not that I go around attacking people, it wouldn't be on. The way I react to other people around me suffering because somebody is 'having a go', and my faculties tell me so, is that I will hit out. I will do everything in my power to stop that suffering.

Some people will say I am wrong in what I do. I am sorry but I am governed by my feelings, if I feel I should do it, then I will not suppress it. I have had some funny situations in circle; they were not funny at the time. Once to help a close friend, I did a conjuration of the ruler of Jupiter, Bethor, the intelligence. I was summoning and commanding to appear etc. when all of a sudden the room went completely black, bearing in mind I had four quarter candles, altar candles, a lamp and a red light for manifestation, and the room went completely black, I went from summoning to 'Oh, please come, thank you very much.' It worked ... it worked in the end. I think it works on a respect basis, if you respect them they will likewise respect you. It is like working with fire; if you don't treat it with respect you are going to get burned.

Interview with Jayne from Northampton

How do I protect myself? What I tend to do is do a general protection every night. I usually start off with the kid's beds and surround them with a yellow or a golden light. Instead of just enveloping, I do a swirling motion. It starts at the end of the bed and swirls around completely, then I fill in all the gaps, completely covering them in yellow light. I don't know why yellow. It is purity, like golden brilliance to scare anything off really. I do one bed then the other bed. It is like a cocoon. I then do it around our bed, round the floor, completely surrounding it in a sphere, like a cocoon shape.

Then I do the house. I do a pentacle at the top of the house and a spiral down in again, right the way to the foundations. Because we are in a maisonette, if you think that something was to hit at the maisonette and you only do your two floors, it is not going to help if something hits the flat below. I do the foundations; I completely miss the people in the flat downstairs because I don't like them, so I just go, foundations, up the wall and up from there. I fill in the gaps as well.

Then the car. With the car I do a cushion effect, so that if anything went to nudge it, it would make an extra bumper all the way over it to give it a bit of rebound. I worry about cars spinning round the corner and clipping it. I just try to give it extra protection.

Me, I don't worry about me so much. I only do it if I feel threatened. When you walk somewhere you sense things, and then I will bang it up. I surround myself in light and radiate it out. Like a radioactive field, I push it out from the body as well, so if anybody had a go, they have to push through the aura, the golden light, and they have to get through that before they can get through to me. It is an added protection. I usually take an aggressive attitude as well. I am never out on my own anyway, but if I was and I felt threatened I would bang that out, but bang aggression with it as well. It tends to do the trick. Stride purposefully. I put my head up, and give off aggression, pure aggression. Not eye to eye contact, but making sure people are not going to mess with me.

Psychic attack; in the home we put seals on the mirrors and on reflective surfaces. We protect the house from the physical with pins and things under the carpets and all that. But with reflective surfaces we draw a pentacle on them. We had a couple of funny things with mirrors; oppressive feelings more than anything which we couldn't figure out. We had guarded the windows, the doors, the mirrors and we found out the problem was coming through a light bulb. When we found out we used salt water and traced a pentacle over it. It did the trick.

The house; we put a seal round it. We put the pins down, the windows are sealed with drawing pins; we put a triangle round the windows with two at the edges and one at the top because it is usually reflective surfaces you have trouble with. We bang that up as well - just to be extra safe. The house is in an envelope. It tends to be at night when you have problems. I don't know if that is just because people think of night as the witching hour or just because you feel it more. You are weak; if you have a cold or flu you feel worse at night because your resistance is lower.

Psychic attack - we've had a few, I think. You are not sure. We have so many coughs and colds anyway. If people are hitting out at you, you feel lower than normal. If I know it is a definite attack sometimes I will light a candle, not necessarily to hit out at anyone, just to ask for protection.

Another thing I like to do is project the force from my hands. If I know someone is having a go, and I know who it is, I will project the energy from my hands. It is more of a ward off, a warning. I project the energy out, like the radiation thing, the aura. It is like a buffer. I tend to do the same sort of thing if I know someone is having a go, just to protect me and keep it away full stop.

We have had a few attacks, usually it is just feeling drained, not as if someone is feeding off you, I wouldn't say it was a vampire. If someone is hitting you it is usually over something petty; they are jealous, they are envious of what you have got. It annoys me. Instead of spending all that energy in hitting out, why can't they use it constructively and make their lives what they want them to be. I have never understood that. They will be so jealous and petty that they would rather hit out at you to take away what you have got. It is a bit Catch 22 really.

There was one night when me and Bill went to bed and I was doing the protection, and there was something up there. I always start at the roof and do the pentacle there so that all the energy comes from the pentacle just above the flat and comes out over the flat and protects it. I said to Bill 'Have you put anything up there?' and he said he hadn't. There was something up there. At the time I had a gorilla as my guardian. The thing up there was a great big spider. It's legs were coming over the windows. I thought 'That's weird.' I didn't know if it was good or bad. It might have been a natural reaction, but you know when a gorilla starts beating it's chest? Well it started doing that.

My first reaction was to send the gorilla off, and it started pummelling the spider which eventually went. It was strange and I kept thinking, was it there to help us or was it there to hurt us? You are never really quite sure, you have got to trust your instincts. If something sets off alarm bells - go for it. If you have a guardian, send it off to do the business, or light a candle or project the energy. The key to protection ... if you are ever in a situation that could be really dangerous, like a magical working and there is a full scale attack whilst you are in there, with love everything is possible.

With me and Bill, if things get a bit hairy, usually we sit together and link hands, and the two of us project the energy out. Love is very powerful. We have never really had much trouble. There have been atmospheres ... things on the side. We do have actual house guardians, but they tend to have appeared on their own. There is one who lives under the stairs and there is one that stands on the landing of the stairs. It is dark there, but doesn't feel oppressive. If you go downstairs at night it doesn't feel bad. If we go away for weekends we set the house guardian, and the other two seem to be fixed as well.

Interview with Anne from Stourbridge

For protection I have got my guardian, my dragon. He is always on my right hand side, looking over my shoulder, ready to pounce if anything should happen. He is the guardian of the house as well. I leave him there sometimes if I am going out.

I use a cloak as well, which is when I don't want to be noticed ... invisibility! The cloak is made of heavy black cotton with a hood - a big hood. I use this when I am out in the street and see somebody I don't want to talk to. It is to hide under.

I have got salt on the windowsills. I have spiky plants on the windowsills too, for protection. I have got my pennies under the carpet by the front door to protect me against going short of money.

Psychic attack is something I would handle if I came up against it, but it is not something I have planned for.

During astral travel I came upon 'Uhhr', he was quite nasty but I don't think he was threatening, just forthright and very demanding. He wanted me to go with him and wasn't going to take 'no' for an answer. He was like a gnome and I met him in the woods. He suddenly appeared by the side of me. He was only about half my height and he had got no hair. He had an old face but a baby face at the same time. I asked him his name and he said 'Uhhr'. He was tugging and pulling me but I pulled away.

Three months ago I went back to the cave which is where I very first went ages ago. There was a man there who was very protective. All I could see was that he had bright blue eyes like sharp specks, I went back there and he took me further back into the cave and told me that this was my hidden depths that I would have to face up to. His name was Jemoriah (Jem-or-ea). He told me to come back when I felt capable of facing the things I had got to face. There has been nothing that I would say had been threatening.

In circle there has been nothing more than uneasy feelings, when you get that shudder down your back but there is nothing there or you are not sure what it is. There have been things happen which I can't explain, but I haven't looked on them as threatening. There was the smoke that time, that rose up by the altar when we were watching television. There were some figures by the front door, the night that the door was left open, and after we had calmed and settled ourselves down a bit, Carl walked into the hall and there were two figures standing there by the front door. They were very hazy - not clear, he did a banishing pentacle and they just went. There has been nothing really bad that I have had to cope with so far, I daresay there will be.

Once during meditation I saw an enormous house, a large porch dominated the front, supported by two large pillars. I looked out over the fields and it began to rain. The sky darkened and I began to run to a copse for shelter. I reached a clearing but it was not empty. A massive spider was sitting in the middle laying large, white shiny eggs, and that frightened me, you know what I am like about spiders! I stood transfixed until the spider moved. I was hoping that if I didn't move or make a noise it wouldn't notice me. It didn't luckily. That wasn't very nice because it was enormous, it wasn't like a big house spider it was about the size of this room. It was big. That is what I do a lot, if I come across something that frightens me I tend to try and blend into the background and hope it doesn't notice me. It finished laying the eggs and went. It wasn't baby spiders that came out of the eggs, it was flowers. This was creative visualisation, I didn't want it to be spiders.

If we are going out we always draw a pentacle on the front door and ask for protection, especially since we found the door open. The cats are good protection as well, especially Cerne. Merlin wears a pentacle on his collar. We actually did a blessing in circle for protection. Cerne is a proper witches cat, he prowls round the house and goes outside and walks around the house at night. I can see him, with his tail up in the air as he watches.

I know that I can cope with any attack that might happen, I have the power to sort anything out if it should happen.

Interview with Carl from Stourbridge

To protect the house when we go out we set the guardians or my own personal guardian. There is also a spiritual wolf there as well, which prowls around when we have been away on holiday or for the weekend. There are the cats as well. We have got three cats. Cerne does a really good job. He goes out of the front, walks around, comes in the back and just sits on the fence watching, as a good familiar does.

The first experience I ever had of funny things happening was a long time ago in Bexhill. I was babysitting for my High Priestess at that time and watching television. This apparition appeared from the back of the telly and started taking shape. It was the biggest cobra that I have ever seen. It took shape out of the mist and must have been about four feet across. I thought it was going to destroy me. I heard their eldest son coming up the drive on his motorbike and I was out of the house and gone. That turned out to be something she had set for me to give me an experience and to see what my reaction would be. My reaction was 'where's the andrex?'.

There have been other times, one of them was in circle. It was not so much an attack but to let me know that he was there. He stood right in the middle of the circle about four feet from the perimeter where the candles were. The whole right hand side of my robe just caught fire and went up in flames.

Personal protection ... I use several forms; a shield, a cloak. I have even visualised solid steel walls, and words of power, things like that. I have never been under a serious attack. There have been instances where I have known that somebody is having a go, and there have been lots of little elementals flying around. I have fed it and fed it on negativity to give it power and to see what is happening and then based my attack on that.

I use a lot of frankincense. If I feel that something is not quite right in the house, I will burn some frankincense and that clears it straight away. There are no two ways about it. I close all the windows, throw the frankincense on the burner, let it all build up then open the windows and it just pulls it straight out. Everything is light and good again.

Protection, well we had a visitor one Saturday night who was sleeping in the spare room. A friend of a friend. Anne saw two red dots on the radiator in our room and I saw them too. Anne thought it might have been the reflection of the buttons on a cardigan. It wasn't until about two weeks after, that she realised there were no buttons on the cardigan and the red dots were red eyes. The explanation that she got from a friend was that she took the form of a panther to watch over us whilst that particular person was in our house. Protection takes many forms, sometimes you don't even realise that it is being done.

I have witnessed psychic vampirism where the individual hasn't been aware that they were doing it until it was pointed out to them.

Sometimes if I am doing any deep meditation I visualise something that means security to me, something like a teddy bear. I wrap myself in a plastic bubble with a tube leading from it, enveloping the teddy bear or what have you, which gives me the protection as well. That is, I suppose purely psychological protection. It still works. I can't bring to mind any instance where there have been major attacks.

Many years ago when I was first drawn towards the occult and witchcraft, 'in the dabbling days' would be the term. Something happened and after the dabbling days were over it was serious. I found out by investigation that there was someone pretty close to me who was, not consciously sticking pins in anything, but the thoughts that were directed towards me were not very good. It was a conscious thing in that way, but the individual was not realising what they were actually doing. That was, I suppose, a pretty major attack, because things did start to fall apart. When I realised this, the thoughts were just sent back and it stopped.

Protection as a whole, or generally speaking is belief. If you believe in yourself and that you can handle any situation in a spiritual sense, that is half the battle. I have battled astrally where I have personally instigated them on an astral level. I have come away with a bloody nose once or twice. But in a physical sense, on a physical plane there has not been much effect. I have had a cord, but not the classical silver cord as it were. It was like some of these illegal wrestling matches where they have a chain manacle and are chained to the ring. It was like that but was around my waist so I could be pulled back from any immediate danger that I was facing.

Cords have played a big part in anything like that, now I think of it. There was one time when I had to protect another person astrally whilst they were engaged in an astral battle, like an all-round defensive thing; making sure that nothing else was creeping in or stepping from behind as it were. I have always been confident in myself. I have an attitude that I am able to handle things like that and to recognise them. That may sound presumptuous, as there may have been things that I haven't recognised for what they actually are.

I have always investigated on a physical level first and if there was nothing there, then it was obviously coming from a spiritual or psychic level. We have had incidences on a physical level where neighbours have been having a go and I have instigated things in a magical sense, and it has worked. We have actually seen it working. Tangible things have happened. Because of what I am, and my belief and faith, I think that that is probably the main protection I have. Belief and faith in the Goddess and the God and the other powers that are with them. I do believe that is the main protection for me, and it does work.

Back in the early days when I was still looking for a direction, I went to spiritualist meetings and there was one guy, who I suppose actually started my training. I was at his flat one evening and he had a phone call calling him out. He asked me to go with him to someones house. We got round to this girl's house and things there had got horrendously chaotic. They had been using a ouija board with letters on paper and a glass. The glass was all over the room. It wasn't just on the table, it was everywhere, up and down.

My friend put his hand over the glass and it stopped, he took his hand away and it was off again. He had to physically pull the glass back to the table and keep his hand over it. I forget the words that he actually spoke, but he said a few words and the glass stopped. He did a quick banishing ritual and everything was more or less back to normal, a lot of atmosphere, panic and fright was left. That was a real thing and shows what can happen if people play around with things they don't know about and don't take the precautions they should in the first instance. That was scary, really scary. It was also an eye-opener to the things that can happen and still do.

Interview with Louisa from the Welsh Border

Odd things used to happen to me when I was young, but they were not really psychic attacks.

I once knew two men who both had the same forename and surname. One was elderly, had suffered a stroke and was in a wheelchair. The other was a young man in his early thirties and in good health. One night, I had gone to bed and sat up to read a book, I put my book down and the light was still on. The room started to go very grey and the walls faded out. It began to get darker and darker and I felt intense pressure all over me. I thought I was going to die. I thought that something had happened in my body and I was actually going to die. I remember thinking that this was what death must be like. I couldn't breathe and I could hear my heart beating very fast, very loud.

The sound seemed to be coming from outside my body. I then felt a sensation of pressure on my neck which got tighter and tighter and was actually very painful. I couldn't breathe and started to panic and then everything really went black. All I could think of to do was to pray. I didn't know much about psychic self-defence or the occult at that time. My parents were spiritualists and the only thing I could think of whilst panicking was to say the Lord's Prayer in my head. As I went through it I felt a woman's presence; I had been told once by a Spiritualist medium that I had a guardian who looked after me, whose name was Sheila and I had been told that she was my spirit guide. I felt a cool hand on my forehead and the pressure on my neck started to ease off and the darkness started to recede. I was half sat up in bed and the light was still on. I felt very drained and I was sweating, but I was cold, very, very cold.

I thought I'd had a nightmare and woken up. I was so frightened that I couldn't turn the light off and I repeated the Lords Prayer another ten or fifteen times. I must have fallen asleep then. When I got up in the morning I told my Mum that I had had this really bad dream when I thought I was going to die and was being strangled by something. It wasn't hands, but the feeling of being choked by something.

When I came home from school (I was in the sixth form at the time) I went into the kitchen and my Mum said 'Sit down, I have some very bad news for you'. She had heard on the local radio that this man we knew had died. She was very upset, and I assumed she meant the older man who was in a wheelchair. 'No', she said 'young Bob'. I was really shocked. Bob had hanged himself the night before. I felt very faint when she told me because the time of death had been estimated at between eleven and one-thirty in the morning. This was about the time I had experienced my 'nightmare'. It was quite frightening that I had picked up his distress, terror and feelings.

I first used psychic self-defence when I was having problems with a teacher at school. To stop myself dreaming about it I would imagine myself inside a mirrored sphere so that any bad vibrations that were sent towards me would be reflected back to wherever they came from.

I used to say prayers a lot, although I am not a Christian and have never been a church goer. I felt that there was a lot of power in certain prayers and I was almost addicted to Psalm 23. I knew it by heart and I would say it to myself, feeling that there was a lot of power in the words. Protective power. I used to pray to Mary rather than to God. Maybe that was a leaning then towards a Goddess form and she was the only one I knew. The Mother figure.

When I started reading things, I would use the idea of the Pentacle and blue light in the aura. I would visualise myself surrounded by blue light with the Pentacle making a seal at the top.

In the house, I haven't got seals as such, on the doors and windows. I have got a charged area around my house, which actually includes part of next door as well, their side of the adjoining wall. It circles the garden, front and back, the path down the side and the adjoining wall. It is like a dome rather than a circle over the whole house. There aren't any individual seals on the entrances. I re-charge this every so often, when I feel the need. It occurs to me that it needs doing again sometimes. If I feel that someone has tried the locks.

About a fortnight ago, I was lying in bed, and began to draw this area around the house in blue light. It is the blue of electricity, like the colour of a blue spark. I imagine that it is an electrical seal and if anyone tried to get in, it would shock them; not to hurt them but to scare them away. It is like a shield or a force field. I have never had anyone breech that barrier until recently. I renewed it then. It hadn't been done for about a month. It wasn't until you started to write about psychic self-defence, that I thought that I must do that. If I don't feel threatened I tend to leave it because it does take quite a lot of energy. If anyone lives on their nerves they tend to push their aura out all the time. This is why you get so tired if you are nervous or worried all the time. It was breeched by something, I don't know what.

It seemed to start a couple of Saturday's ago on Bonfire Night. We were lying on the sofa, Simon was lying on his back and I was squeezed along the edge, and I was talking to him. He wasn't listening, but was looking at something and as I turned to see what he was looking at we both saw a very bright flash, like an electrical spark or a powder flash. We both said 'What was that!' and jumped up and rushed into the hall, where the flash came from.

We thought something was on fire, we looked in the kitchen and up the stairs and there was nothing at all. No smell of burning or after effect at all, just a flash. We were a bit unsettled, but not unpleasantly so, we didn't feel threatened at all. It was quite exciting really. There was no weird air about the place at all so we settled down again.

About a fortnight ago I was on the telephone to Simon, I had been out and it would be about two-thirty in the morning. I heard a very loud crash from upstairs, like something had fallen over. It was very loud and I went to have a look, and nothing had moved at all. There was no disturbance at all. It was the kind of crash that was like a bookcase falling over. Both of my cats were outside so it wasn't them. I was a bit unnerved but I calmed down again and let the cats in, then went up to bed. There was a silence in the house, a tangible silence, not just the normal silence of night time. The air was thick with silence.

I sat up in bed and tried to read. The older of the two cats came up the stairs and stopped on the landing, and was staring at the door of the room where I had heard the noise. Her hair stood on end and her tail was bushed out and she was staring at the door, growling and hissing. The younger cat came up and seemed terrified. She shot into the room with me and got under the duvet, trembling. She climbed into my arms and she is not the sort of cat that normally does that. I was hardly daring to breathe, thinking that something dreadful was going to happen.

After a while things seemed to relax a little and the older cat started to scratch at the door, wanting to go in. I plucked up all my courage, opened the door, went into the room and put the light on. The cat was sitting in the middle of the room, sniffing and staring around her, but not fluffed up. The normal sounds started appearing; I could hear traffic and the odd noises of night, and the freezer and the heating. The noises I hadn't heard at all. I realised that what I had heard before was a very unnatural silence.

I went to work and was fine until it was time to go home. I didn't want to go back to the house in case something else happened. I had a feeling that something was going to happen. I got in the car to drive home and all the way from work to home, the electronic central locking in the car kept locking and unlocking itself. I was starting to feel really nervous and I asked out loud for whatever it was to stop, and it did.

I called my guardian and imagined him in the back seat. I arrived home and rang Simon. I didn't want to stay in the house on my own. I could feel this menace and it was cold. The radiators were all red hot and the rooms were freezing. I went round to Simon's house and he came back with me and brought some candles and incense and things. He was going to work a banishing and sealing for me in his own style, which I don't know anything about. I felt so drained. I had no energy at all, it was as if someone had taken my batteries out. All I could do was sit. Simon actually said that the rooms were cold, he could feel this and knew something was happening.

Then someone who I have had problems with actually turned up out of the blue. Simon answered the door, and this person didn't ask if I was in, just asked if I was all right. He was sent away and then about twenty minutes later we could hear noises upstairs - odd little bumping noises. We went to check if it was one of the cats, but found one was outside and the other had been with us all the time. We did the banishing and it seemed to lift. I found myself writing. I had been writing my diary earlier and had been writing stuff I couldn't remember writing - it was really dreadful stuff about Simon which was not actually true. He reads my diary, and was going to read this, the things that had been put. It was very strange.

When he came downstairs he asked what I was writing. When I looked at the paper I had been writing the persons initials over and over again. It was like a sigil of the initials. That was really strange. Then I felt that I had got to go to have a bath and wash my hair. I felt dirty and full of static electricity which was attracting bad things to me. I felt as if I had soot and smuts all over me. I had a shower and felt so much better. Since then things have been O.K. I haven't had any letters of phone calls from the person who I was having trouble with since then.

Interview with Simon from the Welsh Border

If I am attacked, I tend to become powerful; much more than I am normally. I don't have the concentration to hold a sphere or a blue bubble or whatever, so I do the ripples in the water. I centre myself first, then visualise ripples of blue light pumping out. If there is an entity I visualise it being bounced away and finding it hard to get through. If it is troublesome then I visualise it being crushed by the ripples to the size of a marble, then I see it disappear or exploding. This has only failed about twice. As I said, I don't have the concentration to hold a bubble and with this, I can just keep pumping it out.

I don't have trouble with elementals. I am very elemental rooted anyway, as you know. They honestly don't bother me or play with me at all. If they did I would tell them to 'sod off' and they would go. I haven't been in a position where I have had to defend myself against them. If I ignore them they get bored and go away, they don't get close enough for me to touch them.

In terms of what I call the power elementals, the big ones, the ones with greater consciousness than the general run-of-the-mill household ones. I find them in the woods, I don't find them anywhere else. They probably are nature spirits. In my local woods there are these dark earth elementals which I visualise as wraiths. They can be quite big and have an ebbing and flowing type of sensation around them. There are lots of different ones up there. There is a very big one in my local woods, everyone I have taken up there has felt it. It came and talked to Joyce and she said it was about thirty feet tall and masculine. It is the most intelligent of the lot. When it is there everything else disappears. You know when it is coming because everything else goes quiet. I don't know what it is. John thinks it could be Herne, but I am not sure. I would like to talk to it, and try to get a reaction, but it doesn't stay long.

Many people would probably try to get rid of these things, but because I go there such a lot, I have got used to them and they don't bother me. Some people might think they were being attacked when these things are actually playing games. They have never hurt anybody as far as I know; but they will trip you up. They won't play games with you if you have not contacted them in the first place, if you know what I mean. I don't know if it is me, or if it is the woods, but I will see the things that are there, and other people will pick them up, which is quite unusual. I think some people see astral and some people see elemental and sometimes the same thing. I won't mention them and then someone else will. It is weird really.

Psychic vampires; I am so sealed anyway. I am a very sealed person both aurically and mentally as you will see from my behaviour sometimes. I sense when they are doing it and just seal off, so they can't get any power. I suppose it is like squashing the aura in and putting it almost inside the body. It feels denser and that works for me. As I said before, I can't use a bubble, so I soak up the energy and then add my own power to it and blast it back. I am not sure of the ethics of it.

When I was having trouble with those people who had read books about voodoo and were working rituals, they were pumping energy at me and a friend. I tried to protect the car with a bubble, but couldn't hold it for long and it seeped through. We went up to the woods, and we linked our energy, tapped into the ground, drew energy from there and blasted it straight back. We never heard from them again. So that worked for me. I move like a reed in the wind (talking Chinese now). If you can absorb their energy you are hitting them with that. It is like Martial Arts - you are using your opponents force to unbalance him. It is a waste of time for me to bounce their energy off and then send my energy out after them. Half my energy would be gone before I had started.

The Banishing ... there was something already in the house that had got past the normal seals. I made up an incense of lots of different energy levels, low stuff like mugwort and patchouli and poplar and some high stuff like lavender and frankincense. I wafted the smoke about, especially by the windows and doors - filling the house. Everything the smoke touches gets pulled apart. It is very simple, that is all you do. It fills the environment and really works. The problems that Louisa was having were not elemental but more astral and were disrupted and then pulled apart. At the time I was ill with the 'flu, I really felt too sick to do much more, I didn't have the energy. By the morning everything was back to normal. Incense cleanses everything. Unfortunately a couple of elementals got bottled as well, so I will have to apologize about that. It was completely unintentional.

BIBLIOGRAPHY

A Modern Herbal, Mrs. M. Grieve, F.R.H.S.(1931 Jonathan Cape)

Gerard's Herbal

The Gardeners Folklore, Margaret Baker (1977 David & Charles)

The Great Book of Magical Art, L.W. de Laurence (1915)

Earth Dance, Jan Brodie (1995 Capall Bann)

MAIL ORDER SUPPLIERS

HERB SUPPLIERS

Baldwins,
173, Walworth Road,
London, SE17.
(Herbs, gums and resins)

Culpeper Ltd.,
Hadsstody Road,
Linton,
Cambridge,
CB1 6NJ.

Oak Cottage Herb Farm,
Nesscliffe,
Shropshire.
(A wide selection of fresh, potted herb plants available by mail order or personal visit)

NEW AGE SUPPLIERS

Sacred Moon,
27, Wyle Cop,
Shrewsbury,
Shropshire,
SY1 1XB.
Tel: 0743 352829.
(Crystals, Incense Burners, Books,Jewellery, etc.)

Index